Rabbi
Ralph
Messer

MW00341697

THE
VOICE

Hearing God's Voice with Clarity, Consistency & Confidence

Pneuma Life

PUBLISHING

THE
VOICE

Pneuma Life Publishing
P.O. Box 885
Lanham, MD 20703
301-218-8928
Internet: http://www.pneumalife.com

This book or parts thereof may not be reproduced in any form, stored in a retrieval system, or transmitted in any form by any means electronic, mechanical, photocopy, recording, or otherwise without prior written permission from the publisher, except as provided by the United States of America copyright law.

Copyright © 2001 by John Webster

Unless otherwise noted, Scripture quotations in this book are taken from the Holy Bible, New International Version®, Copyright© 1973, 1978, 1984, by the International Bible Society. Used by permission of Zondervan Publishing House.

Printed in the United States of America
ISBN: 1-56229-183-1

Back cover photo courtesy of Ruth Berry
Signature Images, Panama City, FL
(850)271-9114

Acknowledgements

There are a number of people who were instrumental in making this book possible and without whose help these truths would never have made it onto paper.

To my publisher at PneumaLife, Derwin Stewart. Your continual encouragement and support were invaluable. Our relationship began as a divine appointment, developed into a working relationship, and has grown into a friendship.

To Marsha Capo for your editorial ability. You labored selflessly to make my raw thoughts into something enjoyable to read.

To Nancy Justice. Your editing put the polish on and made the final product ready for the presses.

To Guy and Robyn Bouchard, Dan and Rebecca McKinney, and Rick and Mary Catherine Weller, who provided me with hideaways to write.

To Patrick and Paul Weaver. God made you unique even though you are identical twins. It was from you that God taught me about the "twin voices" within each of us. To Patrick for your loyal friendship and the love of your family for mine.

To Bishop Hamon. You gave me opportunity to hear God's voice for myself. Co-laboring with you for the past twenty years has been an honor.

To all of those who financially supported me while I wrote this book. Your faith in this message while it was yet unseen speaks deeply to my heart.

To Greg and Suzie Williamson. Your special support and friendship means so much to Mary and me. Your confidence also motivated me to get this book finished!

To my wife, Mary. Because I value your opinion highly, your encouragement was second only to God's.

To the Lord, without whom none of this would have meaning.

Introduction

What would you do if you could have your own personal hot-line to heaven? You could talk with Almighty God just like you talk with a friend. What would you want to ask Him? What would you talk about? Consider the possibilities if you had the special ability to hear God's voice just as clearly as you hear human voices. Now imagine if you could talk with God like this anytime you wanted? Would it change your life?

How would your career be different if God gave you guidance in your workplace? How would your marriage benefit from God's counsel and insight? How would your family improve if God advised you about your children? Would you be a stronger Christian if God revealed His destiny for you and then showed you how to fulfill it? How would it feel to have an intimate, vibrant relationship with the Lord? All of this—and more—is possible simply by learning how to hear God's voice with clarity, consistency and confidence.

Are you ready for your life to be transformed?

Hearing God's voice is easy! God has enabled us to communicate with Him and it can be effortless. Why then, have so many Christians struggled for so long to hear God's voice? One reason is that they haven't learned to recognize it. This book is dedicated to providing you with a clear and detailed description of God's voice within you. Once you know what it sounds like, you can distinguish it from the voice of your heart. Learning to tell these two voices apart is a quantum leap forward in confidently hearing God's voice.

Over the course of church history, we have been taught how to hear from God in many ways, including through the Bible, through preaching, and through godly advice. We have learned that God can speak to us through circumstances, through a friend, even by a supernatural phenomenon. We can classify all of these ways as external because they come to us from outside ourselves. Many excellent books have been written about hearing from God through these external sources.

Still other books have focused their attention on God's voice within us. They teach about quiet meditation, "feeling led" and how to "be still and know that I am God". They lay a strong foundation for hearing God's voice within us, but they stop short of a clear description of what His voice sounds like.

We are blessed to have the writings of so many devout Christians to help us hear God through both internal and external sources.

This book can be the next step in your journey to hear God's voice. It is an advanced and detailed revelation of God's voice within you. You will find out about the three "imposters" to God's voice that sidetracks many. You also will read, in detail, what the voice of the Lord sounds like. You will learn the four ways God communicates within us and determine which language God uses to communicate with you personally.

You will discover how to shift from slowly hearing God through circumstances to quickly hearing Him speak to you directly. You will learn about the languages that angels speak, the languages God speaks, and the languages that were given to men at the tower of Babel.

Of course, God doesn't always speak. Yet when He is silent, it often isn't by choice but because we have given Him reason not to talk with us. As we understand what has caused Him to stop speaking, we can take corrective action so that God will speak to us once again.

Some Christians are concerned that they may be deceived when trying to hear God's voice. They worry that a demonic voice may masquerade as God's and mislead them. Under certain conditions this can happen. We'll discuss these conditions as well as provide solutions so you can safely open yourself to the voice of the Lord.

A new phase of your journey is about to begin. Rejoice that God wants to speak to you—via your own personal hotline to heaven. You are about to discover how to hear His voice with clarity, consistency and confidence!

Table of Contents

Acknowledgement
Introduction

1 WE ARE DESIGNED TO HEAR GOD'S VOICE

"**D**id you hear that?!" My wife's worried voice woke me from a deep slumber. It was the middle of the night, but Mary had my full attention. I don't know about you, but 3 a.m. creaks never inspire much courage in me. People often remark that such sounds are "just the house settling." I don't know about the house, but to me it's always "un-settling."

I strained my ears, half expecting to hear the sound of footsteps. "I thought I heard Melody," Mary said. Our fourteen-month-old daughter occupied the room at the other end of the house. Again I listened, again all was quiet. Satisfied there was no one in the house that shouldn't be, I turned on the baby monitor on our headboard. I went rigid as I heard the voice of an adult woman in Melody's room. Myriad thoughts flashed through my mind:

"Someone's trying to steal our baby!"

"But it's such a friendly voice..."

"It's so familiar."

"It sounds like our next-door neighbor, Terry."

"Why don't I hear Melody?"

"Terry sounds like she's talking on the phone."

Then it hit me, our baby monitor was picking up Terry's cordless phone next door!

Somehow our monitor and Terry's phone were on the same frequency and we were listening in on her conversation. Then the big decision came, should we continue to listen? My wife and I voted.

One said yes, the other said no. We turned off the monitor, but I'm not telling which way we voted!

If two devices are on the same frequency they can hear each other. If they are not on the same frequency, they cannot communicate with each other. Similarly, if a person has experienced hearing loss in a certain range of sound, or frequency, they won't be able to hear within their "lost" frequencies. I have lost the ability to hear certain high frequency sound in one ear. When I'm in bed with my good ear against the pillow, I can't hear the alarm clock. Humans cannot hear a dog whistle because the frequency is too high for the human ear. Besides, everyone knows that a dog can't whistle.

When God made the universe, He created everything to communicate on His frequency. Like Terry's phone and our baby monitor, we are on the same frequency with God so that we can hear His voice. Our ability to hear God is because God carefully designed the human race with this ability.

Serendipitous Discovery vs. Creating by Design

Some things are discovered by accident. We stumble across them unintentionally, only to find something remarkable and many times valuable. A very different process occurs when something is developed intentionally. It is carefully thought out and then produced. I refer to these two different processes as "serendipitous discovery" and "creating by design."

Serendipitous Discovery

Serendipity is defined as "making fortunate and unexpected discoveries by accident."[1] The story of how the Post-It Note came into being is a classic example of an unintended invention[2]. Many amazing and useful things are happened upon unintentionally—vulcanized rubber, potato chips, Silly Putty, penicillin and so on[3]. We might use words such as accidental, inadvertent, fortuitous, even miraculous to describe serendipitous discovery.

Creation by Design

Creation by design is very different. In this process, the creator begins with a particular need or goal in mind. After coming up with a design, they then manufacture something that fulfills the need or achieves the goal. This process is intentional rather than accidental and may often require great effort to achieve.

The incandescent light bulb is an example of creating by design[4]. Inventor Thomas Edison began with a final goal in mind and experimented with different materials to produce the desired effect.

The magnificent Gateway Arch in St. Louis is designed to such exacting tolerances that the final section could not be put in place until the eastern leg was sprayed with water, cooling it down from the morning sun. When the metal cooled and shrank, it matched the western leg and the keystone section fit perfectly.

God Creates

Creating by design is not just for mankind. God is a Master Builder. Everything that exists was created by Him. Colossians 1:16 (NIV) says "For by Him all things were created: things in heaven and on earth, visible and invisible, whether thrones or powers or rulers or authorities; all things were created by Him and for Him."

Have you heard the story about the scientists who met with God? With all the recent advances in bio-engineering and cloning, the scientists felt they had a pretty good handle on creating life. They approached God and told Him they didn't need Him, that they could create life all by themselves.

"How about a challenge?" God said. "You go first," they replied. God scooped up some dust and made it into the form of a man. He then breathed into him the breath of life and made him a living being. Now it was the scientists' turn. They got down on their hands and knees and began to scrape together some dust. God interrupted and said "Hey, go get your own dirt!"

I have always felt that the real question for evolutionists is "If you believe life evolved from cosmic dust that developed into amino acids, then protein and finally life, where did the dust come from in the first place?" The bottom line is that everything has a starting point, a time when it first began to exist, and that takes us back to God. He created all things (John 1:3).

God Creates by Design

When God created the world, He carefully thought through every detail. Romans 1:20 tells us, "For since the creation of the world God's invisible qualities...have been clearly seen, being understood from what has been made." This indicates that God carefully designed and engineered all of creation so that it would testify of Him. It's like the world is God's giant billboard advertising who He is.

In order for the natural world to testify of Him, God carefully crafted it so that the message it would bear would be pure and clear.

Romans 1:20 makes this very point by saying "God's invisible qualities...have been clearly seen, being understood from what has been
made..." The word "made" translated is poiema from the verb poieo,
"to make," which means "that which is manufactured, a product, a
design produced by an artisan." Poiema emphasizes God as the
Master Designer.[5] We might think of Him as an artist with creativity, an engineer with precision, or a planner with a blueprint.

Other Scriptures illustrating that God created by design include:

*How many are your works, O LORD! In wisdom you made them all; the
earth is full of your creatures (Ps. 104:24).*

*When I consider your heavens, the work of your fingers, the moon and
the stars, which you have set in place (Ps. 8:3).*

*From heaven the LORD looks down and sees all mankind; from his
dwelling place he watches all who live on earth–he who forms the hearts
of all, who considers everything they do (Ps. 33:13-15).*

Examples from the Natural World

Nature is full of God's design. Birds, for instance, possess an amazing respiratory system that gives them the added oxygen they need to
fly, allowing them to receive fresh air both when inhaling and exhal-
ing. Their unique, creative design produces twice as much air available than would be possible if their lungs were designed like ours.

Sperm whales are the world's deep diving champions, diving
10,500 feet (or two miles!) into the ocean while holding their breath
an incredible ninety minutes. How can they accomplish this remarkable feat even though they're mammals that need to breathe air?
Because God poieama-ed (made) them this way. They can store oxygen in their lungs, as we do, but they also can store extra oxygen in
their muscles. The sperm whale's physiology is so well-designed that
it doesn't get decompression sickness or "the bends" like humans
would.

We are Designed by God

Not only do birds and whales demonstrate God's incredibly creative design, so do we. God poiema-ed (made) us. He designed us as
an artisan would. Psalm 139 says we are fearfully and wonderfully
made. Ephesians 2:10 calls us God's workmanship (poiema). Isaiah
43:7 declares that God formed and made each of us. Zechariah writes
that He formed our spirit within us (Zech 12:1). Who we are,
including our abilities, is the result of God's blueprint. He made the
human race with purpose and by design (Eph. 2:10).

God created our many amazing abilities. Our posture of standing upright is inherently unstable. Our high center of gravity, the shape of our body, and the relatively small amount of surface area in contact with the ground (our feet), would ordinarily make us subject to falling. Imagine how difficult it is to stand a child's doll upright. Yet God designed our skeleton, muscles, and inner ear to work together, controlled by our brain, to give us this wonderful ability.

God designed our soul with equally remarkable abilities. Unlike animals, we have the capacity for humor, creativity and imagination. We have a sense of history that transcends our own lifetime. We can project what might happen in the future. If a human baby and a chimpanzee baby are raised together under exactly the same conditions, only one of them will learn to speak.

God Planned Before He Created

Consider how God occupied Himself before He began to create. The Bible is clear that God is eternal, having existed forever in the past. He is both the Alpha and Omega, the First and the Last, the Ancient of Days. These titles remind us that as the "Alpha," the "first" and the "ancient," He has always been—He has no birthday!

He was Alone Forever, Planning

We don't know for certain what God created first. It may have been angels or it may have been the heavens and the earth. Regardless of what He created first, from that point in time backward, God existed alone throughout all eternity past. Nothing existed other than God. What do you suppose He did? How did He occupy Himself and pass the time? I believe God planned. I believe He carefully thought out everything He would create and what would happen as a result of creation. The Bible tells us that He numbers every hair and that a falling sparrow does not escape His attention.

This means He had all eternity to think through every detail of our existence. Before He began to create, He carefully designed every aspect of creation with His infinite imagination and knowledge. Nothing was left to chance. Every detail was considered. God created all that exists according to a predetermined blueprint that He laid out in eternity past. He then followed His plan, manufacturing or producing according to a design produced by an artisan (Rom. 1:20).

Creating by design has a very interesting application to hearing God's voice. At the beginning of this chapter I told the story of our neighbor's cordless phone and our baby monitor being on the same frequency. God created everything to communicate on His frequency, so everything hears His voice. This is a result of the way in which He designed us. John 10:27 (NKJ) tells us:

"My sheep hear My voice, and I know them, and they follow Me."

God Doesn't Lie

Regardless of your life experience, God's Word is true. If He says it, you can believe it. Numbers 23:19 says, "God is not a man, that he should lie, nor a son of man, that he should change his mind." In the same way, Jesus only spoke absolute truth. He never lied, not even a small white lie.

God Repeats Himself for Emphasis

Every word of the Bible is "God breathed" and important, but how does God draw attention to certain points in His Word that are of special importance? In our modern world of printing and publishing, there are many ways we draw attention—we can underline, highlight or italicize. We can increase the font size, make it bold or all capitals, or change the font style.

Yet God didn't use any of these to draw attention to His Word. His method for emphasis is repetition. If the Lord says something once, we should give it great importance in our lives. If He says it twice, we should stop and carefully consider it before moving on. If He says it three times, fall on your face and don't get up until you know that you have heard and understood!

Jesus tells us in John 10:3 that we hear God's voice:

To him the doorkeeper opens, and the sheep hear his voice; To him the doorkeeper opens, and the sheep hear his voice; and he calls his own sheep by name and leads them out.

He repeats himself in John 10:4 (NKJ):

And when he brings out his own sheep, he goes before them; and the sheep follow him, for they know his voice.

Then a third time in John 10:16 (NKJ):

And other sheep I have which are not of this fold; them also I must bring, and they will hear My voice; and there will be one flock and one shepherd.

Finally, a fourth time in John 10: 27 (NJK):

My sheep hear My voice, and I know them, and they follow Me.

God wants to capture our attention and let us know with great certainty that we hear His voice. He designed the whole human race with this capability. We have been "created by design" to hear His voice.

When God created the universe, He designed everything with the ability to hear and respond to His voice. We are all on God's divine communication frequency. He made us that way. God spoke to the animals and told them to pass before Adam so they could be named. They heard and responded to His voice.

> Now the LORD God had formed out of the ground all the beasts of the field and all the birds of the air. He brought them to the man to see what he would name them; and whatever the man called each living creature, that was its name. So the man gave names to all the livestock, the birds of the air and all the beasts of the field (Gen. 2:19-20).

In a similar way, it was God, not Noah, who called the animals into the ark. Noah and his family had already boarded when the animals arrived. Noah didn't round up the animals and drive them into the ark. Rather, he went into the ark and the animals came in to him. This was a result of God directing them.

> Noah and his sons and his wife and his sons' wives entered the ark to escape the waters of the flood. Pairs of clean and unclean animals, of birds and of all creatures that move along the ground, male and female, came to Noah and entered the ark, as God had commanded Noah (Gen. 7:7-9).

Even bugs respond to God. Just prior to the well-known verse of 2 Chronicles 7:14 we read,

> When I shut up the heavens so that there is no rain, or command locusts to devour the land or send a plague among my people, if my people, who are called by my name, will humble themselves and pray and seek my face and turn from their wicked ways, then will I hear from heaven and will forgive their sin and will heal their land.

God talks to bugs and they hear and respond.

Perhaps you don't consider yourself a giant of the faith. Maybe you don't feel you are as spiritual as you should be. Surely though you have something more than a insect! If animals and bugs can hear God's voice then surely you and I can hear and respond to God's voice.

We Hear Because We are Designed to Hear

God created all mankind with the ability to hear His voice. It is not because of your individual ability, but because of His universal enablement. We hear God's voice not because we are more spiritual than others or have a special anointing. We don't have to pray, fast or sequester ourselves in order to hear Him. We hear His voice because God designed and fashioned within every man, woman and child the ability to hear His voice.

Just as a television receives a T.V. signal because it was designed and created to do so, we hear God's voice because we are designed and created to. This takes all the pressure off us. No longer do we have to feel worthy. No longer do we have to be good enough. We don't have to be a giant of the faith, nor do we have to discover any secret formula. We hear—we all hear—because we are designed to hear. Even if you don't believe you hear God's voice, you are still hearing. God doesn't lie, He says you hear the voice of the Good Shepherd—and you do!

Profession

Make the following profession by reading it aloud. Let this moment be an anchor for your faith that you hear God's voice.

"God created the universe by design. Everything in it was created for a purpose, and has special characteristics to fulfill its purpose. God created me to hear His voice. He fashioned within me everything I need in order to hear His voice.

He designed all of humanity with special abilities, one of which is to hear Him. Because I am a member of the human race and because I have been created with this special ability, I hear His voice.

My ability to hear God's voice is not based on my own goodness. It is not because I view myself as being spiritual enough to hear Him. It is not because of my works or my own individual talents. My ability to hear God's voice has nothing to do with me as an individual. My ability to hear Him is not based on a deliberate effort on my part, how hard I try, how much conscious effort I expend, or even how aware I am of hearing Him. My ability to hear God's voice is because of the Lord and the way He made me.

I agree with God's Word, and I profess that I HEAR GOD'S VOICE!"

In the blank space provided below, sign and date this profession. You will have this moment to look back on forever as the time when you agreed with God that you hear His voice.

(Your Name)____*Beverly D. Fouts*_____

(Today's Date)____*February 10, 2005*_____

2 Speaking God's Language

The young man startled me. He had just blurted out that he already knew he would marry a woman he had just started dating.

He prayed late one night about his relationship with her and asked God if she was the one God had chosen to be his wife. Then he told me, with excitement in his eyes, that he asked God to show him a shooting star if she were the one. He looked up and there it was, his sign from God streaking across the sky.

Soon after that he told the young woman, who didn't see things quite the same way. Not surprisingly, she soon broke up with him. Yet he remained convinced she was the one. Several years later she married a godly man and as far as I know, is still happily married.

Not only was this young man's way of discerning the mind of God immature, he was wrong. He was looking in the wrong place for his answer.

Looking for the Supernatural/Spiritual Voice

Doesn't it seem as if we want God to speak in a supernatural or spectacular way? How often have we asked Him for our own special sign from heaven? We long for an angelic appearance with a message from God and think that hearing God's voice must be a miraculous experience. Perhaps it's because God spoke to the Israelites from a smoking mountaintop. Perhaps it's our fallen nature or our religiosity that tells us it is something different from what we have experienced.

God does remarkable things to communicate with us. You might know someone who experienced a supernatural event where God miraculously answered a prayer, solved a problem or communicated His will. The Bible records many such events. He spoke to Moses out of a burning bush. He appeared to Joshua as the Captain of the Hosts. His voice thundered from heaven at the baptism of Jesus. He appeared as a blinding light to Saul on the road to Damascus. Christians often find themselves longing for God to speak to them, supernaturally and theatrically.

It is clear from the Bible that God speaks this way, but if we aren't careful a lifetime can be wasted away waiting while nothing happens. The truth is, these awesome experiences are often once-in-a-lifetime occurrences that most people never experience. Most of the time God speaks in ways that are more common yet just as important.

Fine china vs. Everyday Dishes.

My wife uses our fine china and crystal on special occasions, but our everyday dishes are those we use, know and with which we are familiar. God sometimes speaks in awesome ways, but this is His "special occasion" voice. His everyday way of communicating with each of us is so common and comfortable that it doesn't seem super-natural, spiritual or spectacular. While some have been waiting for the burning bush others hear from the Lord continually. These are the people who sought to hear and learned to recognize God's "every-day" voice.

We've been speaking God's language all along and didn't know it. It's amazing how animals communicate. The dance of the honey bee, the song of the humpback whale, the flashing of a firefly, even the ter-ritorial marks of the wolf are just some of the ways animals convey a message. There is even evidence that marine animals use biolumines-cence to communicate[6] . Of all His creatures God gave humans the most unique gift for language. He also gave us other forms of com-munications such as writing, drawing, music, facial expression and body movement.

His Language in His Image

When man was first created, we find him talking with God in the Garden of Eden. Because God recently created Adam, he had noth-ing of his own. He did not have time to build, create or gather any-thing. Everything that surrounded him and everything he possessed belonged to God. Even the language he used when he spoke with the Lord was God's. The important thing to understand is that man and God could communicate via talking, or language. Language first belonged to God—it is the language God spoke.

Language and communication are part of the nature of God. The first act of God recorded in Scripture was through speech.

In the beginning God created the heavens and the earth. Now the earth was formless and empty, darkness was over the surface of the deep, and the Spirit of God was hovering over the waters. 3 And God said, "Let there be light," and there was light (Gen. 1:1-3).

He passed this wonderful ability along to us when He created us in His image. Yet it wasn't just a language He passed along, but His language! God gave us many things that first belonged to Him. He gave us HIS Son, HIS image and HIS way of communicating.

God shared vocabulary with us. God gave man diverse earthly languages at Babel (Gen. 11). Angels have their own languages that differ from ours:

If I speak in the tongues of men and of angels, but have not love, I am only a resounding gong or a clanging cymbal (1Cor. 13:1).

It should be no surprise to learn that God has His own languages. However, He has shared these languages with us so that we may communicate.

God's languages include dreams, visions, speech, thoughts and impressions. I categorize these into three basic styles: visual, auditory and kinesthetic (sensing). For example, dreams and visions are visual. Speech and thoughts are auditory. Impressions and feelings are kinesthetic. God is not the only One who uses these forms of communication, we do too because God gave us these languages when He created us.

Every part of us uses these God-given languages. God created us with a spirit, soul and body. Each part of our being uses these languages. Below is a table showing how each part of our being uses these forms of communication.

Styles of Communication

	Visual (Seeing)	Auditory (Hearing)	Kinesthetic (Sensing)
Body	Body language	Speech	Touch
Soul	Dreams, Imagination	Thoughts, Inner Voice	Impressions
Spirit	Visions	Still Small Voice	*Pascho*[i] Feeling

Using this table, we see three parts of our being use the God-given languages of seeing, hearing and sensing. In the case of hearing, our body uses it to hear speech. Our soul uses it to "hear" our thoughts. Our spirit uses it to "hear" God's still small voice within us. Using the book of Psalms as our guide, we find instances of hearing by each part of man: body, soul and spirit.

The body:

Come and hear, all who fear God, And I will tell of what He has done for my soul (Ps. 66:16).

The soul:

Tremble, and do not sin; Meditate in your heart upon your bed, and be still (Ps. 4:4).

The spirit:

I will hear what God the LORD will say; For He will speak peace to His people, to His godly ones; But let them not turn back to folly (Ps. 85:8).

Unlocking Your Ability to Hear

The languages we speak are God's languages that He gave to us when He created Adam. All three parts of our being speak these languages in their own way. We are familiar with talking to ourselves (hearing), dreams and imagination (visual), and impressions (feelings). These are ways in which our soul uses God's languages. Because these are comfortable to us, we can easily learn how our spirit man uses them and quickly learn to communicate with God spirit-to-Spirit!

You don't have to learn an entirely new way of communicating to hear from God. Neither do you have to wait for a supernatural manifestation. Your spirit can use the same languages with which your soul is already comfortable. You can become skillful at hearing from God!

3 Recognizing God's Voice

Several years ago when our first child, Jonathan, was a baby my wife suggested we take turns getting up with him during the night. I don't think I'm an inconsiderate sluggard, but the idea of getting up in the wee hours of the night didn't strike a resounding chord in me. I reasoned that because she was nursing Jonathan, she was up anyway so why bother me? But it was hard to make my point with a woman who had been pregnant for nine long months and had labored and delivered just weeks earlier. Sensing my fate was sealed and any additional complaining would only serve to highlight my shortcomings, I quietly agreed to crib duty every other night.

I would change Jonathan's diaper, and then lay him in bed next to Mary for his feeding. When he was finished, I tucked him back in bed and made sure he was sound asleep before falling back into bed. Mary said she could feed Jonathan without really waking up and this would give her a much-needed night's sleep. I would get a full night's sleep on my night off.

I didn't understand how she could nurse him without waking up, but I knew my understanding wasn't important—my cooperation was. I was a first-time dad and decided that on my nights of crib duty I would perform my responsibilities with great care and diligence.

One night, after returning to bed, I tossed and turned restlessly until I finally drifted back to sleep. The next thing I knew I was flying. The foot of the bed passed underneath my airborne body and my feet outstretched to meet the floor rushing up at me. In the fraction of a second that my flight must have lasted, it amazed me that my transition from sleep to wakefulness had taken place several feet above the ground. My musings abruptly turned to panic as I realized what had catapulted me out of the bed: the sound of Jonathan choking.

With my adrenaline pumping wildly, I bounded through the house in twenty-foot leaps. I landed in Jonathan's room and peered intently through the darkness at his still form cozily nestled in his blankets. Then I heard it again... the sounds that had catapulted me from bed. A slow smile spread over my face as I realized my son was only gurgling in his dreams. I slumped over the edge of his crib, completely drained and then dragged my weary body back to bed. Such is the life of a new parent.

Crib duty taught me many things, including how to change a diaper and return to bed without ever fully waking. I also became aware of "selective hearing." When it was Mary's night to get up with Jonathan, I would sleep the night through and never hear a thing. But when it was my turn, I could hear the rustling of baby sheets from the other end of the house. It soon dawned on me that when I was responsible, I placed great importance on hearing Jonathan. Yet when it was Mary's night to take care of him, my sleep was blissful.

Selective Hearing

God gave us the wonderful gift of selective hearing. This ability allows us to sort through the myriad bits of information that bombard our senses—and we're not even totally aware that we're doing it. We can give our full and undivided attention to the most important matters at hand without getting distracted by everything going on around us.

Just think of your local shopping mall at Christmastime and all its sounds. Among them are common noises such as assorted conversations, the rustle of packages, the waterfalls, the strollers with squeaky wheels (and sometimes squeaky babies!). Added to this are noises unique to the holiday season: music competing from store to store, frantic shoppers short on gift ideas, sleigh bells, harried elves, and coaxing parents at Santa's North Pole. While we may find this cacophony of noise an assault on our ears, we may be totally unaware of the individual sounds involved.

Selective hearing is so effective we may not be aware it is even happening. A fellow shopper may ask "Did you hear how rude the salesperson was to that customer?" Absorbed in thought, we might answer "No." But if they heard it, we did too. The same sound waves that traveled through the air and vibrated their eardrums also vibrated ours. Our ears converted these vibrations into electrical impulses and transmitted them to our brain. We heard, but we did not pay attention. Our God-given gift of selective hearing filtered out the voice. Physical hearing works twenty-four hours a day, awake or asleep, without any effort on our part. Our eyes have eyelids, but our ears don't have ear lids. God created us to hear.

I have discovered my own special phenomenon that involves some sort of skip pattern of sound waves. Yet it only occurs once a week— every Monday night during football season, particularly when the Miami Dolphins are playing. Any other time I can hear Mary's voice from the kitchen, "Honey, please take out the trash!" But during Monday Night Football I hear nothing! She calls me repeatedly, but I hear only the voices of Al Michaels and his broadcast buddies. People tell me this has nothing to do with sound waves skipping over my head, yet it is another example of selective hearing. Whatever the cause, I'm just glad it works.

Value, Not Volume

A key to selective hearing is determining what is important. Going back to the example of the shopping mall at Christmas, we may not consciously notice the waterfall or the rustle of packages. But we will detect the frightened cries of a lost child crying for mommy, particularly if that's our child! The difference is not that one sound is louder than another or even more imposing. It is all a matter of what we consider important. Selective hearing is an issue of value, not volume.

It is important to understand that we hear all of the sounds around us. However, if we are absorbed in thought or our mind is otherwise occupied, we are aware only of sounds that hold some importance to us. We notice much more when we are attentive to our surroundings. In either case, sound waves are traveling through the air and strike our eardrums so that we "hear" everything.

This is why I heard Jonathan's baby gurgles the night I awoke in midair. When it was my turn to get up with him, I placed great importance on hearing. When it was Mary's turn, I slept undisturbed. Again, it is a matter of value, not volume.

This is a God-given ability. He created it within us so we could concentrate on what is important or interesting to us without being interrupted by the trivial. Can you imagine what it would be like if every random noise arrested your attention as completely as Jonathan's midnight gurgles did mine? Without the ability to filter out unimportant sights and sounds on a subconscious level, our lives would be nothing more than a series of distractions.

Selective Hearing Overused

The downside to selective hearing is that we can sometimes block out things that are truly important. This can happen when we incorrectly identify an important sound as unimportant. This happens to me at Wal-Mart when I drop off my car in the auto department for an oil change and go about the rest of my shopping while they do the work. The auto department is supposed to page me when my car is ready. Though I have done this many times, I have yet to hear my name over their public address system even though they assure me that they did page me.

I seriously doubted them so I decided to put it to a test. I dropped off my car and began my other shopping as usual. This time I kept a careful ear out for my page. I quickly realized that Wal-Mart's public address system is in constant use with advertisements, employee pages and other meaningless (to me) announcements. I would never get any shopping done if I carefully listened to every announcement. I discovered that I had so effectively blocked out these announcements that even when they said something important, I subconsciously assumed it was unimportant and ignored it. Incidentally, I still can't say for sure that they ever paged me!

The Great Dilemma

We know from the passage in John 10 (discussed in Chapter 1) that God's Word promises we hear His voice. Even though we know this, we may often feel that we don't hear God, at least not as much as we would like.

How often have we needed His wisdom or answer to a question? How often have we cried out for Him to speak to us, but heard nothing? When this happens, a dilemma faces us. If our experience doesn't line up with God's Word, we may feel frustrated or that we are failing in some way. The answer to the dilemma between God's Word and our experience can be a fairly simple one.

Selective Hearing and Our Spiritual Ears

We have spiritual ears just as we have natural ears[8] . Selective hearing functions on both a natural level and on a spiritual level. How often have we taken a dire need into our prayer closet, only to find the heavens were as brass? How often have we asked God to speak to us, but heard nothing? Our natural ears always hear and we don't have to do anything special to cause that to happen. Our spiritual ears work the same way. They always hear and require no deliberate effort on our part.

When God speaks, we hear. Just as with our natural hearing, selective hearing in the spirit realm is dependent upon what we think is important. It is a matter of value, not volume. However, if we have never learned to identify God's voice correctly, then when He speaks to us we misidentify Him. We may think it is our own desires, or vain imaginations, or even our mind wandering. When this happens, our selective hearing blocks Him out just as effectively as it does all those Wal-Mart announcements.

Silencing our thoughts when we pray is another way we suppress His voice. We may find thoughts going through our mind as we pray. Thinking they are "just me," we block out God's voice and leave our prayer closet believing we didn't hear Him! If this is happening, one of the biggest revelations for getting a breakthrough in hearing God's voice may be understanding selective hearing!

Recognizing: The Key

In Chapter 1 we established that we hear God's voice. If you are a member of the human race, God is speaking to you and you are hearing Him[9]. The key is not to learn to hear, but to learn to recognize what we hear. If we knew with absolute certainty that it was God speaking to us, we would give Him our full, undivided attention. But what if we don't know what His voice sounds like? When He speaks, we might very well think our desires, imaginations, or wandering thoughts are talking. On the other hand, if we learn what His voice sounds like, then we could come to the place where we hear God's voice clearly, consistently and confidently.

Recognizing: A Learning Process

Samuel was a remarkable man. He is the first full-time major prophet in the Bible. Other prophets came before him, such as Moses, but Moses' major work was that of a deliverer. Besides Samuel's prophetic ministry, he also trained other prophets. He established the schools of the prophets and raised up the sons of the prophets. He anointed kings. Samuel also wrote parts of the Bible—1 and 2 Samuel. If anyone heard from God, it was certainly Samuel—but it wasn't always that way.

Samuel's mother, Hanna, had been barren. After crying out to the Lord for a child, He gave her Samuel. Hanna dedicated the young boy to God and then took him to Eli the priest to be raised. Samuel was still a child when God started speaking to him. The first occurrence happened late one night after everyone had gone to bed. The

Lord called Samuel by name.

First Samuel 3:4 says that Samuel ran to Eli, thinking it was the priest who had called him. Eli, not knowing about God's call to Samuel, sent him back to bed. Three times God called, three times Samuel went to Eli, and three times Eli sent him back to bed. It was on the third occasion that Eli realized it was God who was calling Samuel. This time, Eli sent Samuel to bed with these instructions:

> Go and lie down, and if He calls you, say, 'Speak, LORD, for your servant is listening (1 Sam. 3:9).

Indeed the Lord spoke to Samuel. He told him about the corruption of Eli's sons and the judgment that was coming to them.

We glean three important principles from this event regarding God's voice. First, God's voice sounded fatherly and familiar to Samuel. He thought it was Eli. Second, Samuel was not able to recognize God's voice instinctively. He had to learn what it sounded like. Third, Samuel's teacher was a man, not the Lord Himself.

God Uses Others to Teach Us

The Bible tells us that the Holy Spirit is our Teacher:

> But the Counselor, the Holy Spirit, whom the Father will send in my name, will teach you all things and will remind you of everything I have said to you (John 14:26).

John 16:13 says in part:

> But when he, the Spirit of truth, comes, he will guide you into all truth . . .

Some have misunderstood this verse, believing it means that God will do the teaching without the help of man. Some take this to an extreme and refuse to receive from others, developing an unteachable spirit. When teaching seminars in churches on hearing God's voice, I frequently ask those in the audience who are Christians to raise their hand. Often everyone raises their hand. I then ask them to leave their hand raised if they became a Christian because of someone sharing the gospel with them. Again, most have their hand raised.

Then I ask the clincher: "If the Holy Spirit leads you into all truth, how is it that a person shared the gospel with you and led you in the born-again experience?". With a touch of humor I also ask how many have been baptized in water and if another person led them in that experience. The obvious point is that the Holy Spirit often uses human vessels to lead us into truth. While He can, and often does, lead us into truth directly, He also uses the preacher's preaching, the counselor's counseling, and the teacher's teaching. We must resist the wrong belief that God will only teach us directly by His Spirit. The prophet Samuel is a testament to God using people to teach us to hear God's voice.

Learning Involves Practice

I sometimes call this next verse "the scripture that sounds unscriptural." It contains a truth that many people don't view as spiritual. This principle sounds too natural, yet it is a primary key to spiritual development. It is often "hidden" because of our super-spiritual approach. It is found in Hebrews 5:14. The King James is a difficult rendering, but we will start with it and then look at other translations:

But strong meat belongeth to them that are of full age, even those who by reason of use have their senses exercised to discern both good and evil.

Let's focus on these two phrases: "by reason of use" and "senses exercised to discern."

We have spiritual ears, spiritual eyes, and a spiritual sense of touch. We must exercise these spiritual senses by using them. The writer of Hebrews is telling us this when he says, "by reason of use." When we exercise our muscles in a workout, they respond and become stronger. So it is with our spiritual senses. The more we use them, the keener they become. This is a process, and it takes time, but it is very effective.

The New International Version (NIV) translates Hebrews 5:14 as:

But solid food is for the mature, who by constant use have trained themselves to distinguish good from evil.

As we constantly use our spiritual eyes and ears, we train ourselves. This is the part that seems too natural for many people. They would prefer that God appear in a dream or vision, take the coal from off the altar and touch their mouth. Wouldn't it be wonderful to have an overwhelming spiritual encounter with the Lord and receive a diving impartation that enables us to hear His voice and speak for Him? This happened to Isaiah, but it is a rarity. If the Lord has done this for you, then you are one of few who have received this type of sovereign visitation and impartation. For the rest, the Hebrews 5:14 process is how we develop our spiritual senses. It requires us to apply ourselves, to be diligent, and to be trained.

Notice the NIV says that we are trained "by constant use." The New American Standard and Revised Standard say:

But solid food is for the mature, who because of practice have their senses trained to discern good and evil (NAS).

But solid food is for the mature, for those who have their faculties trained by practice to distinguish good from evil (RSV).

In both cases, practice trains our senses. Wow! Who would have thought that hearing the voice of the Lord would involve training and practice? Because we didn't know to practice, we haven't been growing. Many are still crawling when God is trying to get them to walk and run.

Practice Involves Mistakes

I cannot count how often I have missed something special because I was afraid I might make a mistake. It's been said that we learn more from our failures than from our successes. Yet in the church there is often intolerance for those who are learning, and we certainly wouldn't encourage them to practice. In sports, we not only tolerate practice, we expect it. Musicians understand the value of practice and accept that they will make mistakes as they strive for excellence. It is part of the process of learning.

How much more should we pursue excellence in the things of God? Athletes are willing to practice to be the best they can be. Should the people of God do any less? The household adage "practice makes perfect" has truth to it. Paul addressed this when he told the Corinthians:

Since you are eager to have spiritual gifts, try to excel in gifts that build up the church (1 Cor. 14:12)

Even Jesus learned through the things He experienced:

Although he was a son, he learned obedience from what he suffered (Heb. 5:8).

Giving ourselves, and others, the right to practice and make mistakes is important. We must pursue excellence even when it means that we may learn best by finding out what not to do. We must develop an atmosphere of acceptance, tolerance and respect for each other.

When we seek to affirm and edify each other, even as we are learning, we will find more people taking chances.

A Proper Time and Place for Practice

The athlete and musician know there is a time for practice and a time for performance. We expect them to practice and learn from their mistakes. We also expect them to be ready for the performance and excel without mistakes. The sour notes are for the practice hall and the beautiful music is for Carnegie Hall. It is not that one is wrong, but that both are good and have their right place.

As we pursue excellence, this lesson will serve us well. Practice is healthy and needful, but it also has a proper place. Once we move into the public forum and begin sharing what we heard from God, we need to be certain we are speaking accurately. The church service is not the place to practice. When dealing with the precious lives of others, we can't afford to make mistakes. The diamond cutter and the heart surgeon dare not make mistakes, but both had to develop their skill in a practice environment.

We can practice hearing the voice of the Lord in many ways. I know of many pastors who provide their congregations with special services and settings for such practice. We can even practice in the privacy of our own heart.

Whether you practice with others or alone, whether formally in church or informally in your daily life, practice is the only way to bring about success!

4 Telling Apart "the Twins"

How embarrassing to not recognize a close friend. It happened to me several years ago during a visit to Tuscaloosa, Alabama.

I was returning to a church where I had ministered several times before and was friends with the pastor and many people in the church. The pastor had arranged a dinner at someone's house and I was looking forward to seeing everyone, especially my dear friend, Patrick Weaver. Whenever we came to town, our family always stayed with them. It had been too long since our last visit. Keep in mind that Patrick had an identical twin, Paul, who lived in the same city and attended the same church, but I knew him only by acquaintance.

My family and I arrived for dinner on time. I knocked on the door and Patrick answered…or was it Paul? The man who answered the door was clean shaven—no beard or mustache. Since Patrick was supposed to be there and was clean shaven, I assumed it was he. Yet I thought it might be Paul, even though he usually had a mustache and was not supposed to be there. Something on the inside told me this was Paul.

I considered Patrick to be a close friend, a person with whom I had shared my heart. As I stood at the door, I couldn't tell him apart from his twin. I quickly decided it was Paul, all evidence to the contrary, and said "Paul, it's so good to see you!" He greeted me with a hug and welcomed me in. I was right! Paul had shaved his mustache and had come to dinner without my knowledge. I had correctly told the twins apart.

"The Twins" Inside Us

As Christians we each have our own set of "identical twins" inside us. One is the voice of the Lord and the other is the voice of our own heart. At first these "twins" look and sound alike. No wonder we often ask ourselves in confusion: "Is it me or is it God?" "Is this the Lord speaking to me or am I making it up?" Wrongly identifying these identical twins is probably the most common cause of mistake when learning to hear God's voice.

Distinguishing Between "The Twins"

I once asked Patrick if he had ever fooled his mom. He said it was only possible if he were at the end of a dark hallway, at night, with his back turned and he didn't say anything. Even then it only worked for a second or two. Wow. Why can't identical twins fool their parents? Because Mom and Dad know them—they've spent time together. They know the subtle differences. Both Patrick and Paul are married, but their wives, Candace and Lela, don't confuse them. Once you spend time with identical twins and get to know them well, they become as unique and different as any other two people. I learned this lesson while watching Candace fix dinner. Patrick was helping while I sat on a stool and enjoyed all the delicious smells and intimate surroundings of a warm kitchen and good friends. [Just so you know—I offered to help, but was declined!]

At one point I looked up and saw Patrick's profile and had an earth-shattering revelation. Before I could stop myself I was blurting out: "Patrick! You and Paul do look alike!" Patrick looked at me in a way that questioned my intelligence. Of course, he's a good friend and far too kind to think such a thing, but I sure did. I couldn't believe what I had said. Patrick and Paul are identical twins for heaven's sake. Then I realized I had come to know Patrick so well that I no longer saw him as a twin. I had spent enough time with him that I saw all the subtle differences that make him a wonderfully unique person.

Discerning Between the Voices

I had a revelation in the Weaver's kitchen that night. The Lord showed me how we learn to discern between His voice within us and the voice of our own heart. We do it by taking the time to get to know our "twins." Like a parent, spouse or close friend who can discern the identity of each twin, so can we distinguish between the two voices. It requires spending time with God and tuning our spiritual ears to His voice within us. We must develop a lifestyle of listening, rather than waiting until a desperate need arises. We must listen in every area of our life, not just those areas in which we need answers.

Knowing Each Twin

On another occasion I was ministering at a different church in Tuscaloosa. I was hoping Patrick would come so we could visit, but he didn't arrive until after I had started preaching. It was a small, informal church so I stopped and greeted my good friend publicly. He waved oddly, but I figured he was just uncomfortable with the attention. Then I realized it wasn't Patrick, but Paul. I was embarrassed, but learned a valuable lesson. I had come to know Patrick well enough that I could recognize him. Yet I didn't know Paul well. I was unsure at which twin I was looking. It is odd that if you know only one twin, you may be confused when you see the other.

When learning to tell the twins within us apart, we have to get to know both of them. Not only should we listen to the voice of the Lord, we also must listen to the voice of our own heart. That's right! It is essential we get to know both twins. This means we spend time with both, learning their subtle differences. If we get to know only one twin, we can successfully identify only that twin. When we encounter the twin we don't know, we can again be perplexed and be right back to square one, asking "Is it me or is it God?"

When we understand that we have twin voices inside us, we greatly enhance our ability to hear. We realize that in learning to hear from God, we aren't listening for a new, mystical voice. Instead, we listen for the twin to the voice of our heart. It is familiar and comfortable to us. It is encouraging to know that we don't have to learn a new voice; we have only to recognize God's voice that we have been hearing all along.

5 Imposters

I was raised a Methodist and taught to be very quiet and reverent in church. Yet it wasn't until I was a junior in high school that I became a born-again Christian. It was 1977 and I started attending some very unconventional services due to the widespread influence of the Jesus Movement. I joined countless other on-fire young people at a renovated car repair shop we called God's Garage. We showed up in our tattered jeans shirts and sat on the floor, singing praise choruses and listening to preachers. This would have been totally unacceptable at my Methodist church, but I was a new convert and everything seemed so fresh and exciting.

Sometimes things got out of control. One evening we were listening to a preacher with a confrontational, blustery style. He was telling a story about a young man he had ministered to the night before. The story was somewhat self-promotional, painting the preacher in a very positive light. Suddenly a guy in our "congregation" jumped up and headed toward the platform, yelling "You're a liar!" at the preacher.

Apparently he was the very man the preacher was talking about and didn't approve of the preacher's recollection of events. An argument broke out and the preacher called for the ushers to remove the man, who was now on the platform. Things quickly escalated and a fight broke out. The ushers wrestled the man to the floor, in the process bumping the piano, which rocked back toward the pianist. About this time a man in the balcony yelled "Cast the devil outta him!"

I wondered what I had gotten myself into, but soon learned that the preacher had brought it on himself by not being truthful. In another meeting with the same preacher he publicly berated the sound man because the microphones were giving him trouble. Over the next several years I heard of this man's ministry and discovered him to be rude, egotistical and uncaring. Yet many people thought he was wonderful and actually viewed his angry tirades as being from God.

Misconception that God is Angry

I have met and observed other church leaders who have a similar domineering, dictatorial leadership style. Yet, their followers firmly believe their harsh, critical, demanding leader is acting the way Jesus would. They think that if Jesus walked the earth today, His words would always be brutal and stinging. This view of God reflects their inner belief that He is always angry, stern and serious—a critical God who likes to focus on our weaknesses.

Misconceptions About God's Voice

If God was an angry, harsh, critical God, we would naturally expect Him to speak in an angry, harsh, critical way. Any misunderstanding we have about the true loving nature of the Lord causes us to expect Him to speak in ways that are hurtful to us.

To overcome these misconceptions let's take a look at the Old Testament prophet Elijah. He had an encounter with God on the mountain that illustrates how we might misunderstand the way He speaks. In 1 Kings 19, we find major misconceptions about the voice of the Lord—what I later call in this chapter the three "imposters."

Elijah on the Mountain of Faith

Previously, in 1 Kings 18, Elijah had had a major confrontation with the false prophets of Baal on Mount Carmel and challenged them to a showdown. The terms of the dual: Elijah and the false prophets would prepare a sacrifice to their respective gods. The god that answered by fire would prove to be the One True God and the Israelites would serve him.

Jehovah answered by fire. A major victory was won that day and three important things happened. First, Elijah rebuilt the altar to sacrifice to the Lord. Second, when fire consumed the sacrifice, the children of Israel experienced revival, and renewed themselves to God's covenants. Third, they cemented their commitment by killing the false prophets of Baal.

Elijah demonstrated tremendous faith on Mount Carmel. He believed God would send fire from heaven and consume the sacrifice. As he stood in faith, he saw the power of God.

Elijah on the Mountain of Fear

Jezebel, Queen of Israel, was the patron of the false prophets of Baal. Now they were dead and she lashed out at Elijah. A warrant for his death was issued. Elijah must die.

The order quickly spread throughout the nation. The confidence Elijah felt during the contest with the prophets of Baal was long gone[10] . He hadn't anticipated this backlash and needed a place to hide and to hear from heaven. His flight lasted for weeks and ended on Mount Sinai, the same place where Moses had received the Ten Commandments. Elijah found a cave and began to pray, waiting for the storm to blow over. He didn't have to wait long.

Elijah's State of Mind Blurred His Perception

From inside the safety of the cave Elijah heard the Lord calling him out onto the mountain. Elijah was in a place of fear, despondency and isolation. His fear over the queen's threat caused him to flee for his life[11]. This was not the first time Elijah was the subject of a royal man-hunt[12].

His discouragement may have been the result of fear or the feeling of being ineffective in ministry. The three-year drought, fire from heaven, and the rain that ended the drought were all insufficient to cause national repentance[13]. The nation was still alienated from the Lord. Perhaps Elijah felt that he had done all he could and with a sense of futility said to the Lord "I have lived long enough for thy service, and am not like to do thee any more service; neither my words nor works are like to do any good upon these unstable and incorrigible people."[14]

In a time of fear and despondency Elijah isolated himself. This may have been a pattern for the prophet. Three times he says he is alone when he knows there are at least 150 prophets in Israel, including Elisha (1 Kings 18:22, 19:10, 19:14, 18:13). He apparently didn't seek them out. It was Obadiah, not Elijah, who saved the 150 prophets from Jezebel's wrath[15].

Elijah's emotional state of fear, despondency and isolation blurred his perspective. First Kings 19:10 shows us both his state of mind and how he incorrectly viewed things.

And he said, I have been very jealous for the LORD God of hosts: for the children of Israel have forsaken thy covenant, thrown down thine altars, and slain thy prophets with the sword; and I, even I only, am left; and they seek my life, to take it away.

When we compare Elijah's perspective with the facts presented in Scripture, we find they are almost opposite of the truth. Let's look at each of them:

Elijah's Perspective: "...the children of Israel have forsaken thy covenant"

The Truth: the children of Israel experienced a mass revival on Mount Carmel and renewed themselves to God's covenants (1 Kin. 18:39).

Elijah's Perspective: "...thrown down thine altars"
The Truth: the altar was rebuilt (1 Kin. 18:30).

Elijah's Perspective: "...slain thy prophets with the sword"
The Truth: the false prophets of Baal were killed, not God's true prophets (1 Kin. 18:40).

Wind, Earthquake and Fire

While Elijah was in a state of emotional upheaval God spoke to him. But in between God's comments something interesting occurs:

And behold, the LORD passed by, and a great and strong wind tore into the mountains and broke the rocks in pieces before the LORD but the LORD was not in the wind; and after the wind an earthquake, but the LORD was not in the earthquake: and after the earthquake a fire, but the LORD was not in the fire (1Kin. 19: 11-12NKJV).

In this passage the wind, earthquake and fire are classic examples of how we perceive God's voice to be something that it is not. God was not in the wind, the earthquake nor the fire and didn't use them to communicate with Elijah. Why would He need to? Elijah was a prophet and had received God's messages on many occasions without wind, earthquake or fire. God called Elijah out of the cave by His voice—the wind, earthquake and fire were not necessary.

There are many Christians today who look for God to talk with them via this form of communication. I've labeled them "The Three Imposters."

Imposter #1: The "Wind"

The wind speaks of mystery. We can hear it and see its affect on our surroundings, but we can't see it nor can we tell where it has come from or where it is going.

There are those who think God's voice is like the wind in that it's mysterious and difficult to discern. Who hasn't, at one time or another, wondered what God was saying to them? Who hasn't wanted to dialogue with God as easily as we converse with one another? We assume that only prophets, leaders and spiritual giants hear God's voice. When we struggle to hear from God, we often seek advice from those mature in the Lord or whose spirituality we respect. This attitude is the result of years of prevailing sentiment that those who hear from God best are spiritual and mature.

In reality, we all hear from the Lord very easily. It isn't elusive, difficult to discern, or mysterious. In truth, it is one of the easiest things we can do. But because we haven't been taught how to hear, we often find ourselves seeking but not finding; asking but not hearing. The Bible says "God was not in the wind." Neither is the voice of the Lord mysterious. One of my goals in writing this book is to help believers understand they have the ability to hear the voice of the Lord clearly, consistently and confidently.

Imposter #2: The "Earthquake"

An earthquake is a powerful, physical shaking; an obvious, unmistakable event. A well-known brokerage firm used to advertise "When E.F. Hutton speaks, people listen." There is a school of thought that says if God speaks to you, it will be obvious and unmistakable, and that He will somehow get His point across. The world is full of people looking for signs and omens about their future.

My wife and I enjoy watching romantic movies. One of our favorites is Sleepless in Seattle. Meg Ryan plays a woman engaged to Walter (Bill Pullman), but is obsessed with Sam (Tom Hanks). In one scene, she is trying on her mother's wedding dress and it tears. She tells her mother "It's a sign! I'm not supposed to marry Walter."

The practice of looking for a sign is prevalent in the church as well. Gideon asked God for a sign of His will by putting a sheepskin fleece outside and asking for it to be wet with dew when the ground was dry. This practice is so common today that we have an expression for it: "putting a fleece before the Lord."

God is gracious and He often gives us a sign, but this is not His first choice. Just as a loving father would rather talk with his children than to leave them notes, the Lord would much rather speak to us directly than to show us signs. In the story of Elijah on the mountain we are told "God was not in the earthquake." The meaning for us today is that we don't need a powerful shaking or an obvious sign to help us understand what God is saying. Instead, we can listen to His voice.

Imposter #3: The "Fire"

In the Bible, fire is a symbol of refining and purifying, but phrases such as "hellfire and brimstone" or "the fiery darts of the enemy" make us think of fire as judgment. There are some who see God's voice as judgmental. Nothing could be further from the truth. God's leadership style is based on love and affirmation, not on fear and criticism.

Romans 2:4 (NIV) says it is the goodness of God that leads us to repentance:

Or do you show contempt for the riches of his kindness, tolerance and patience, not realizing that God's kindness leads you toward repentance?

When there is sin in our life, God often shows us His love and kindness to prompt us to repent. He may remind us of all the things He has forgiven us for, and the sacrifice He made for our salvation by dying on the cross. When we see it afresh and anew, when we realize the price He paid and how He has forgiven us, our hearts melt and we turn away from sin. It is His loving kindness that leads us to repentance.

God's voice is not often critical, harsh or condemning. More often, it is loving, compassionate and kind. If we haven't heard God's voice in this wonderful way, it may be because we're in a state of ignorance and perceive it to be something it is not.

God's Still, Small Voice

After telling us that God was not in the wind nor the earthquake nor the fire, 1 Kings 19: 11-12 beautifully declares that our Lord's is "a still small voice."

The voice of the Lord is a "delicate, whispering voice."[16] It is definite and distinct, but it is also subtle. Once we have learned to recognize His voice it can be a whisper that shouts, like the soft, distant cry of a child. In terms of volume it is soft, but it has the ability to cut through the clutter of sound and arrest our attention. This is the way God prefers to speak. He wants us to learn what His voice sounds like so we can communicate with Him in a running dialogue. He would like for us to be so in tune with His voice that the cares of this life and the other voices competing for our attention are parted like the Red Sea and we clearly discern His still, small voice.

Will God Ever Speak in the Wind, Earthquake and Fire?

For every general rule, there are always exceptions. The general rule is that God's voice is not difficult to figure out (wind), it isn't overwhelming or accompanied by a sign (earthquake), and it isn't critical and judgmental (fire). The exception is that God is sovereign and He may speak in any or all of these ways in order to get through to us. If you have experienced any of these types of communication and you thought it was God, don't change your mind now. It may very well have been the Lord. However, God prefers to speak to us by His still, small voice.

Learning to Recognize the Still, Small Voice

How do we learn to recognize God's voice? If it isn't the imposters of the wind, earthquake and fire; then what is it? The next chapter covers what the voice of the Lord sounds like. There is a detailed description of His voice that will help you in knowing what to listen for. Now that we've talked about the imposters, let's move onto the next chapter, "The Real McCoy," where we will learn what God's voice sounds like within us.

6 The Real McCoy

A s I sat in the restaurant and listened to my pastor friend, I couldn't believe he was talking about adultery. He had so much going for him, was incredibly gifted and his advice had helped many leaders, including me.

It was after a midweek service and we were enjoying a nice dinner when he told me about the "other woman." His marriage had been as strong as ever and he was deeply in love with his wife. He had not been pursuing an illicit relationship, but the previous year had been a difficult one in the church and he was battling discouragement. It all began with innocent chats between him and a female church member. Little by little, almost imperceptibly, he began enjoying her company and found himself preoccupied with thoughts about her. It happened so gradually it dulled his senses to the horror of sin.

He didn't even see this "innocent" relationship as unhealthy. In fact, he said, it was nothing more than a problem with his thoughts. Even with this, he was okay when at home. It was only when he was away from home that he felt an attack of impure thoughts. He had no impure contact with her and viewed the whole thing as an attack of the enemy. He decided he needed to guard his thoughts carefully, but was concerned about enjoying her company.

It all came to a head when he was away on a ministry trip and stayed at a hotel. He called her home to thank her for some books she had sent him. During the conversation he realized she had no godly boundaries and seemed to welcome his call and whatever might follow. It was as if the fog suddenly lifted off him and he realized where this was headed. She would definitely be a willing accomplice. The casual innocence was stripped away and he felt himself on the brink of adultery.

The seriousness of the situation hit him full in the face. So this is how it happens, he thought. It kind of sneaks up on you and before you know it you're on the verge of a sin you never thought would happen.

The next morning as he walked down the hotel hallway, he passed a man talking on a cell phone. He overheard him say, "He can get out now if he wants to, but she is going to have trouble stopping it." It immediately grabbed his attention—God was speaking to him! In his valley of the shadow of death, God put this man in the right place at the right time to say the right thing. God was telling the pastor that he could get out of this situation now if he wanted to, but that the woman would have difficulty stopping it.

The message was clear: "There is still time if you act now. She won't stop it, but you still can." Chills ran through him as the fear of God came over him. He cried out in his heart, I want to stop this now!

My friend's story has a wonderful ending. He repented to God and his wife for allowing another woman to captivate his thoughts and heart even though there had been no physical contact or inappropriate conversation. He learned his wife already suspected that this woman was in love with him. The couple prayed together and the episode proved to strengthen their marriage.

External and Internal Voices

God uses many ways to communicate with us. One primary way is through His Word, the Bible. As we read, study, and submit ourselves to His Word, God will cause illumination to come to us by His Spirit, leading us into all truth[17]. God also talks to us through the preacher's preaching and the teacher's teaching. We might classify these methods as "external" because God is using something outside us.

Other examples include godly counsel, creation and the natural world. God can even orchestrate our circumstances to get a message to us. With my pastor friend, God used a man on a cell phone in a hotel hallway. Most often the speaker is completely unaware that God is using them, but we know it's God—not them—who is speaking to us.

This is not to say that God is always talking to us through one of these ways, only that He can if He chooses. Yet they are all outside us. Many books are available on the external ways God speaks to us. In her book *Forever Ruined for the Ordinary*, Joy Dawson identifies twenty-seven ways God speaks to us .

I believe the most common way God desires to speak to His children is when His Spirit speaks directly to our spirit. We can learn to hear, recognize and respond to the wonderful voice of the Lord within us. God wants us to have extended conversations with Him throughout the day, walking in communion with Him, and His Spirit leading us[18].

Recognition is the Key to Hearing

Perhaps the greatest key in learning to correctly hear God's voice is to identify what it sounds like. If it is described to us in a clear, detailed way, then we can learn to recognize it. When He speaks, we can know it is God rather than the voice of our heart. This chapter seeks to describe God's voice with detail and clarity.

I hope and pray you develop a definite sense of God's voice within you. As He speaks, you will know it is Him and focus on what He is saying. We grow in our ability to converse with Him and come to the place where we are communing with Him moment by moment. No longer will we have to have a major encounter in the presence of the Lord to catch a glimpse of what He is showing us. Instead, we can come to the place where we are clearly seeing whatever He wants to show us.

Preeminence of the Bible

God's voice within us is the most frequent way that God would like to speak to us, but it is not the most authoritative. The Word of God, the Bible, is the ultimate authority that judges all other forms of communication. Everything that we believe to be God speaking to us, either within us or through an external source, must agree with Scripture. God speaks to us extensively through His Word. Both as we read and study it, and as we hide it in our hearts. As we study the Word of God and let it become part of us, God will speak to us by causing us to recall a relevant truth out of His Word. Consequently, it would be imprudent to try to be too definite in separating the voice of His Spirit within us from His Word within us because His Spirit often draws upon His Word. When defining God's voice within us,

we must make ample room for Biblical principles and verses that we
have learned and memorized, which He uses to speak to us.

As we study God's Word and let it become part of us, God will
speak to us by causing us to recall a relevant truth out of His Word.
Consequently, it would be imprudent to try to be too definite in separating the voice of His Spirit within us from His Word within us
because His Spirit often draws upon His Word. When defining God's
voice within us, we must make ample room for biblical principles and
verses that we have learned and memorized.

What Does God's Voice Sound Like?

The Bible gives us a few key verses about the sound of God's voice
within our spirit. First Kings 19:12 describes it as a still small voice.
A margin note in the New King James translation calls it "a delicate
whispering voice." It is soft and quiet, yet it can cut through the clutter of sound bombarding us.

Say, for example, you're at the company Christmas party. There are
conversations all around you as coworkers form and reform into different groups. It is a dynamic environment as new people enter and
others leave and conversations continually change. It is impossible
keep up with other conversations as you try to show interest in what
your group is saying. Amid this cacophony, a hushed statement floats
over from a distant group. They said your name and mentioned a
significant promotion that was still secret. You realize what you had
been working hard for all year long is going to happen—a promotion
is on the way.

Important news has a way of cutting through everything else. We
heard it despite the deafening noise around us. This is the nature of
a still, small voice. It doesn't insist or demand to be heard. It is gentle and inviting.

Another way of thinking of the still, small voice of the Lord is by
comparing it with our conscience. They are two very different voices
and have different purposes, but they sound alike. As we reach for
another cookie, our conscience may say "You've had enough."
Sometimes this voice can be loud and insistent, but at other times it
can be soft and easily ignored. We know it is there, but we can turn
away from it if we don't like what it is saying.

The still, small voice of the Lord is often soft and easily ignored,
but it is also definite. If we tune our hearts to hear it, there is no mis-
taking what it is saying. Yet if we choose not to listen we can ignore
it and feel as if it isn't speaking to us.

Three Ways God Communicates

The Bible gives us special glimpses into the nature of God's voice. In certain verses it's as if God draws back a curtain to show us what His voice sounds like when He speaks within us.

A distressing vision is declared to me... Therefore are my loins filled with pain: pangs have taken hold of me, like the pangs of a woman in labor. I was distressed when I heard it; I was dismayed when I saw it (Is. 21:2a-3 NKJV).

This passage contains three ways God communicated with Isaiah in this "distressing vision": touch, sight and hearing.

1.) Touch: Through a spiritual sense of touch, or feeling, Isaiah said he felt God so strongly in his physical being that he compared it to childbirth: "Therefore are my loins filled with pain."
2.) Hearing: Isaiah, through his spiritual ears, wrote "I was distressed when I heard it."
3.) Sight: With his spiritual eyes Isaiah then said "I was dismayed when I saw it."

The Bible repeats these three methods with Saul of Tarsus, who later became the Apostle Paul. God appeared to Saul on his way to Damascus, a bright light blinding him. God sent a devout man named Ananias to pray for Saul. Acts 22:14 records what Ananias said to Saul:

Then he said: 'The God of our fathers has chosen you to know his will and to see the Righteous One and to hear words from his mouth (Acts 22:14).

Spiritual touch is found in the statement "know His will."[19] Paul would need spiritual eyes so he could "see the Righteous One," and spiritual ears to "hear the voice of His mouth."

God gave each of us spiritual senses so He could communicate with us through these methods of seeing, hearing and feeling. Chapters 7 through 15 explore these three methods of communicating in-depth. With a detailed understanding of what it is like when the Lord communicates with us in these ways, we are better able to receive from Him. We are able to engage in the "real McCoy"—the true way God communicates inside us.

7 Dreams, Visions and Trances

For a person like me who has had very few spiritual dreams, this was one to remember!

In the fall of 1992—right after the election of Bill Clinton—I dreamt I was at my childhood home, playing football catch in the yard with President-Elect Clinton. After a few minutes he caught the football, walked over and stood in front of me. He didn't say a word, but I knew he wanted to know what God had to say to him through me. I said several things, but I remember only one of them: "God has chosen you to be president." Then I woke up.

I strongly suspected that this dream was from the Lord, but I was reluctant to believe it for several reasons. First, I wondered "Who am I to have a spiritual dream about the president?" Second, Bill Clinton was not my choice for president and I didn't like the fact that he was God's choice. (Maybe this will please people of both political affiliations, but I fear I have only succeeded in alienating everyone!)

Even though I tried to forget about it, the dream stayed with me for days and was hard to shake off. I called my brother, Scott, who is also in ministry and whose opinion I deeply respect. If anyone thought I was unqualified to have these kinds of dreams, it would be a brother. I invited him to lunch and told him what was on my mind. He listened carefully and took time to think about it. Then he said, "John, I believe there are not many people to whom God would speak about the president. But I believe you're one of them."

I didn't know whether to cry for joy at this affirmation, or cry in frustration because now I had to take the dream seriously. I later discussed it with my mentor and spiritual father, Bill Hamon, who shared the same opinion as Scott.

I never relayed this word from God to President Clinton. Part of this may have been fear, but the bigger part was the realization that the dream, and others that followed, were meant for me, not for others. God was telling me that I was now hearing on a different level. This was difficult for me to accept—it took several similar events for God to convince me that He now was speaking to me on this new level.

In this chapter we'll discuss how God sometimes uses dreams to speak to us. I'll also describe the visual nature of dreams and other visual ways God uses to communicate, such as visions and trances.

God Speaks to Us Through Dreams

The Bible has many examples of God speaking through dreams—to believers as well as to non-believers. Some of the most significant dreams recorded in the Old Testament were interpreted by Daniel and Joseph, but dreamt by the unbelieving Nebuchadnezzar and Pharaoh.

The number of dreams we may receive from God varies from person to person. For some, spiritual dreams are the primary way God communicates with them. Others have very few or none at all. This is not an issue of spirituality, but God's sovereign choosing and a wonderful way to hear from the Lord. However, the recipient needs to guard their heart from pride. They don't want to soil it by thinking they are more spiritual or more favored of the Lord.

Those who have few or no spiritual dreams can take heart. If God isn't speaking to you through dreams then He is probably speaking to you in another way. Find out that "other way" rather than trying to have spiritual dreams.

Dreaming is universal; spiritual dreaming is not.

All of us dream whether we remember our dreams or not. Some people have many dreams while others have very few. Some have spiritual dreams while others rarely do. We should not try to gauge how spiritual we are based on how many dreams from God we have. Nor should we try to make every dream into a spiritual one. For the average person, most dreams are just our heart and mind processing things or working through issues. Some are simply the result of what we ate the night before. These "pizza dreams" can be pretty wild!

Both soul and spirit use the language of dreams. Dreams are a form of language used to communicate thoughts, feelings and messages. Unlike speech, dreams use more than just words. They also include thoughts, pictures, feelings, sounds and symbols. Dreaming is a very elaborate and complex way of communicating. Our heart uses this language to speak to us in the night. These "self dreams" (in contrast to spiritual dreams) allow our heart to ponder things, process feelings, and even explore areas that our waking mind won't allow. "Self dreams" comprise most of the dreams for the average person.

God also uses the language of dreams when He wants to communicate a spiritual message. He may intervene in a "self dream" and insert a spiritual message. The difference in these two approaches is that a spiritual dream is from the Lord in its entirety. A self dream with a spiritual message is a dream that comes from our heart, but into which the Lord interjects a spiritual thought or message. It is important to distinguish between the two. If God adds a spiritual message into a self dream, we wouldn't want to assume that the entire dream is from Him.

The language of dreaming does not identify who is speaking. Every dream is not from God. It may be from our heart or even demonic spirits. We cannot assume that just because a message comes to us in the form of a dream that it's from God. It might be from our heart (self-dream) or from a spirit (demonic dream). It is important that we learn to discern the source of our dreams.

The nature of the dream does not identify who it is from. Some dreams are realistic and lifelike while others are fanciful. Some dreams have strong emotions and others do not. Some dreams are compelling while others are easy to forget. Some dreams are literal and others are symbolic. Some dreams are frightening, others are peaceful. A dream can have any of these characteristics no matter where it originates—with us or with God.

It's incorrect to believe that a dream is from God because it is compelling, or that a dream is from the devil because it is frightening. Dreams must be spiritually discerned. Godly dreams aren't always peaceful, symbolic, or compelling. We must be able to determine which dreams are from God by discernment, not by how they make us feel.

God speaks the language of our heart. The language of dreams is spoken by both the heart and the Spirit. Because both God and our heart speak the same language, it can be easy to confuse who is speaking. It would be easier if we knew that all dreams were from God so we would never be confused, but this is not so.

Other languages that God and our heart share are pictures[20], an inner voice, feelings and thoughts. Many Christians find it difficult to hear from God because they don't realize that both God and our heart share these languages. For example, they may hear a voice on the inside, but not know if it is God talking to them or just idle thoughts going through their mind. We'll cover more of this topic in Chapter 8 and Chapter 10.

Dream Interpretation is a Separate Gift

A pastor friend recently called me for help with dream interpretation. One of his members in a position of responsibility believed God had given them significant dreams about the church. The person wrote out the dreams and their own interpretations and gave it to the pastor. They described the church as lacking in holiness, leadership that was both controlling and passive, and worship that grieved the Lord.

The pastor sent this to me along with interpretations of these same dreams from another member of leadership who has the gift of dream interpretation. Over the years this person had proven his accuracy of interpretation. The pastor had asked his opinion of the dreams without revealing who the dreamer was, the dreamer's interpretations, or the fact that the dreams were about their church. He responded with interpretations that were positive and uplifting. They revealed unique gifting within the leadership, and even spoke of the purpose for the dreamer within the church.

As I consulted with the pastor, the dreams were clearly from God. This gave credibility to the dreamer, but their interpretations were way off. Their inaccurate interpretations could have been very convincing. Had it not been for a person with the gift of interpretation, the dreams could have caused extreme turmoil for the church.

In the Bible, dreamers of godly dreams could not always interpret them. In Daniel 2 Nebuchadnezzar dreamed of the image that foretold four world empires, but he needed Daniel to interpret it. The king also dreamed of the tree cut down, symbolizing God humbling him (Daniel 4). Again he needed Daniel to interpret it.

Joseph interpreted other dreams because the dreamer could not: the butler's dream in prison, the baker's dream in prison and

Pharaoh's dream of the cattle, which predicted seven years of plenty followed by seven years of famine.

A person may have dreams from God, but lack the ability to interpret them. The Apostle Paul addresses this issue in 1 Cor. 14:6-12 when he says that interpretation is vital. He continues in 1 Corinthians 14:27-28 (NIV):

> *If anyone speaks in a tongue, two-or at the most three-should speak,*
> *one at a time, and someone must interpret. If there is no interpreter, the*
> *speaker should keep quiet in the church and speak to himself and God.*

Paul considered it possible for a person to have the gift of tongues, but not the gift of interpretation. Nebuchadnezzar and Pharaoh both sought an interpreter. The lesson for us is that the dreamer isn't always the best interpreter. When an interpreter can be found, dreams can be a tremendous blessing to the church.

God Speaks Through Visions

Occasionally God will open our eyes for us to see in the spirit realm as we do in the natural realm. He did it with Elijah's servant who saw the army of God as flaming chariots. Visions appear just as "real" as the physical world around us. When we see a vision, it is difficult to say whether we are seeing with our physical eyes or our spiritual eyes. God may do a miracle in our physical eyes so we can see in the spirit realm. However, He may make it seem as if we are seeing with our physical eyes when we are actually seeing with our spiritual eyes.

Visions are common in the Bible, but rare in our experience. Visions were a common part of biblical events. While not an every-day experience, they're mentioned occasionally yet matter-of-factly. In our present-day Christian experience, we seem to hear less about them. I frequently ask my audiences how many of them have seen visions. I am careful to explain that I mean seeing in the spirit realm just as they see in the natural realm. Surprisingly, I regularly have a few who have, which causes me to wonder if visions are rare these days or if we just don't talk about them.

Visions are not a language we have, but an experience we are given

In another chapter we talk about inward visions as a common way God speaks to us, using a pictorial language. When God created each of us, He fashioned some of us to see, others to hear, and still others to feel. Educators have explored our style of receiving and call them learning styles. Evidently, our learning style is a result of how God made us. It is part of our very nature. In this sense, it is part of our gifting.

If we are a visual person, God created us with the ability to perceive in a seeing way. When we apply this to spiritual things, we can say that God has gifted a visual person to receive from Him in a seeing way. They can see inward visions as a matter of course when "talking" with the Lord. It is the primary language they use in their communication. This is also true of those God has created to hear and those He has created to feel.

However, a vision is not part of our God-given language. It is not something we can see anytime we choose as we communicate with the Lord. Instead, it is a supernatural and sovereign event God gives us as He chooses. I find no indication in Scripture of anyone who had visions as their usual way in which God "spoke" to them. This distinguishes visions as special events rather than as a usual method of communication.

Let me reiterate that visions are valid and some people are blessed to have them more often than others. Prophets, who were once referred to as "seers," were among those who had them more frequently. However, they are not part of our day-to-day communication with the Lord as are inner pictures and God's inner voice.

God Speaks Through Trances

A trance is a sleep-like state where we have little or no awareness of our surroundings. God used trances to communicate with Peter, Paul, John and Balaam, and perhaps others. Trances are even more rare than visions and occur only a few times in Scripture. In each case the person was drawing closer to the Lord in some way. With the Apostle Peter, he was praying on the housetop of Simon the Tanner (Acts 10:10). The Apostle John had a vision on the island of Patmos, possibly while in a trance "on the Lord's day" (Rev. 1:10). Paul was praying in the temple when he fell into a trance (Acts 22:17). Balaam's trances were in connection to prophesying, where he would get alone with God[21].

Nowhere does the Bible suggest that we should seek to enter a trance or practice meditation to enter a trance. Peter, Paul and John were pursuing God, not a trance. There is no indication that they intended to fall into a trance or in any way induced it. In contrast to this is an interesting combination of facts regarding Balaam. He was a false prophet[22] and a soothsayer who practiced divination[23] . He alone states that he must "go" somewhere to meet with God[24]. This statement, and his practice of divination, infers that he was accustomed to seeking solitude where he would contact the spirit realm. Whether or not this involved a self-induced trance is unknown.

Valid When From God

Though trances are rare in the Bible, and they should not be self-induced, they are nonetheless a Scriptural and valid way for God to communicate with us.

Dreams, visions and trances are some of God's visual languages. Each of these is visual in nature and used by God to speak to us. While dreams can be common, and visions less so, trances seem to be rare. By far the most common visual language is inner pictures, or inward visions, which we discuss in the next chapter.

8 Inward Visions

B elieve me, the last thing on my mind was an angelic visitation. In fact, I'm embarrassed to say my mind wasn't at all on God. It was praise and worship time at a church in Boise, Idaho, and instead of joining the others in worshipping God, I was thinking about last-minute changes I had made to my upcoming message. I thought about the notes I had tucked away earlier in my Bible.

It was then that I looked up at the platform and saw angels. They stood shoulder to shoulder against the wall, facing us. I stared in utter amazement and noticed there were more of them. They stood along the front wall of the church, then down the side walls, and finally across the back. I noticed their height, posture and dress. The three that stood in the center of the front wall were different from the others. They were dressed in gold and their swords were bigger. They were also bigger and taller than the other angels and seemed to be the ones in command.

The other angels were dressed in white. They were physically impressive, but not as much as the center three in gold. All of the angels had swords, but none of them were drawn. As I studied them, I realized they were warring angels God had sent to protect our atmosphere of worship from demons who would like to disrupt it. The angels were definitely no-nonsense and looked very serious about their responsibilities. I could see how demon spirits would think twice before trying anything.

Seeing angels is hardly a common experience for me. I can count on one hand the number of times it has happened. This encounter was quite a shocker. What I saw overcame me and I understand why so many people in the Bible fell to their knees when they saw an angel! That's exactly what I started to do even though I knew Scripture taught against it and that angels repeatedly refused worship.

I was in awe of what I saw. My immediately reaction was to fall on my face in humility and reverence. Before my body could respond, God spoke to me. He showed me my heart. I realized that I was quick to bow to these angels though I knew it was wrong. I saw that I had been untouched by the worship offered to the Lord and had chosen instead to think about the sermon. I immediately repented for my lukewarm attitude toward God and began to worship Him wholeheartedly.

Pictures: A Language Spoken by God and Our Heart

In my seminars on hearing God's voice, I often ask audiences to close their eyes and picture their home. I first ask them to see it from the street, then walk in the front door and look around. I might even ask them to walk through the various rooms and look at the furnishings. When I finish with this exercise, I ask them if they could "see" their home. The response is almost universally positive.

God has given us the wonderful ability to visualize. Clearly the exercise is not God speaking, but it does involve the language of pictures. If the picture is moving and we see it in our sleep, we know it as a dream. If it is a picture we see when we are awake, we refer to seeing it in our "mind's eye." The Lord also speaks this pictorial language and often uses it to communicate with us. God was speaking to me in this language when I saw the angels during the church service in Boise.

It is the same language, but a different speaker

Whether I visualize my home or see angels, it is the language of pictures. In the first instance it is my heart speaking (memory). In the later instance it is God speaking. Yet in both cases, it is the same language. Consequently, regardless who is speaking, it will appear the same to us.

Here again we are looking at "the twins" and trying to tell them apart. We see a picture, but who is talking? Is it God or is it our heart? The first key to knowing when God is communicating with us is to recognize that He will use pictures. These pictures will look identical to the pictures our heart uses to speak to us.

Inward Visions and Visual Imagination

When the Lord communicates with us in this pictorial language, we call it an inward vision. It is a vision because it is coming from God. It is inward because it is happening inside us. When our heart speaks to us in this pictorial language, we might call it visual imagination. Visual because of its pictorial nature, imagination because we are creating an image from our memory (or in some cases from our thoughts or creativity). We also can create these images from our desires, our dream house for example. Inward visions and visual imagination are like identical twins. They look just alike, but they are different.

The chart below illustrates how very different these two are:

	Inward Vision	**Visual Imagination**
Source:	God	Us (memory, creativity)
Nature:	Real, spiritual	Imagined, recalled
Where:	In our spirit	In our soul (mind)
When:	As God chooses	Any time we choose

There are many examples in Scripture of inward visions. Jesus had an inward vision surrounding His introduction to Nathanael. When they first met, Jesus said, "You are an Israelite, and there is no deception in you." He continues, "Before Philip called you, when you were under the fig tree, I saw you." Nathanael's response was, "You are the Son of God! You are the King of Israel!" Nathanael, knowing that they had not seen each other previously, immediately accepts Jesus as the Messiah because His revelation was so specific and accurate.

How did Jesus receive this revelation about Nathanael from His Father?[25] It was through an inward vision. Jesus said, "I saw you sitting under a fig tree." If it had been natural sight Nathanael would not have reacted as he did. It wasn't a vision; otherwise the Bible would have identified it as such as it does elsewhere. It was an inward vision Jesus saw with the eyes of His Spirit.

Saul of Tarsus also had an inward vision. Before his conversion to Christianity, he was a devout Jew who persecuted and killed Christians. On the road to Damascus the Lord appeared to him as a shining light that was so bright it blinded him. Jesus spoke to Saul and he was converted. His friends then led Saul into the city because of his blindness. God spoke to Ananias, a godly man, to pray for Saul so that God would heal his eyes. God gives Ananias instructions about finding Saul saying,

> *In a vision he [Saul] has seen a man named Ananias coming in and putting his hand on him so that he might receive his sight (Acts 9:12).*

While Saul was blind, he saw a vision of Ananias. His natural eyes were blind, but his spiritual eyes were working. He was a blind man seeing. He had an inward vision.

We can take a major step forward in learning to communicate freely with the Lord by understanding how inward visions come to us and by recognizing them as coming from God, not from our own heart. God loves to communicate with His children[26]. One of the most prolific ways He does this is by giving us inward visions. Keep in mind these are simply pictures God places inside us. They may have little or no emotion associated with them so we won't necessarily "feel" like it is God giving us this picture. It may feel as unemotional and unimpressive as closing your eyes and visualizing your house.

One way we can learn to become more aware of inward visions is to pay attention to what we are seeing when we pray. Look inside as you spend time with the Lord. What images are forming? It may be something you are praying about and the Lord is giving you confirmation or greater understanding about how to pray. Other times what we see inside is so completely unrelated to what we are praying that we dismiss it. Before rejecting the picture, allow it to remain as you pray. If it isn't carnal or displeasing to the Lord, it does no harm to leave it alone. Continue to pray and see if the picture becomes relevant at some point.

People who are highly visual may see many inward visions. They may have a virtual movie playing inside them or they may have picture after picture flashing through them. It would be a mistake to try to slow this process or squelch it in any way.

This sort of editing is a chief reason we have difficulty hearing the voice of the Lord. We are quick to discount anything we are receiving by blaming it on ourselves, thinking "that's just me," "I made it up," or "my mind was wandering." By blaming everything we see on our heart or mind, we dismiss it as irrelevant and we never learn to receive from God.

Right about now some of you are saying "That's too easy—if I did that I would see things constantly." EXACTLY! That's the whole idea. God loves to communicate and we can see what He is showing us.[27] Stop talking yourself out of it. It is time to arise in faith and believe so you can have nonstop communication with the Lord!

The natural and the spiritual can combine.

Sometimes this inner pictorial language can overlie physical scenes. For example, you are considering a new chair for your living room. You stand in the room and look at the spot where you would put it. You are seeing a physical scene with your natural vision. Keeping your eyes open and continuing to look at the selected place, you then "imagine" the chair there to see how it will look. You have just over-laid an inner picture upon a physical scene. In this example, the inner picture came from the imagination, but it can also come from an inner vision.

When I saw the angels during the worship service, it was an inward vision overlaid on my surroundings. I saw the church, the platform and the worship team with my natural eyes. I saw the angels as an inner picture from God. I trusted what I saw with my spiritual eyes as much as what I saw with my natural eyes. Both were "real," but only one was physical and tangible. This is the language of pictures.

Discerning Between Your Soul and Spirit

Some pictures we see inside of us are from us. It may be our mind wandering, a lasting impression from our day, or a troubling scene from T.V. burned into our mind. On the other hand, we have to make room for the possibility that some of these images are coming from God. How do we know which is which?

We learn to tell these two identical twins apart through experience and training. Inward visions are easily confused with our imagination and heart. Some people have a strong desire to hear the voice of the Lord purely, without polluting it with their own thoughts and desires. They also may have a fear of thinking that something has come from God when it has not. It is pleasing to the Lord that we honor and respect Him so highly that we are careful and pure in hear-ing His voice.

We wouldn't dare believe something to be from Him unless we knew beyond any doubt that it was so. However, we can misuse these positive qualities. We can become so careful to weed out the false that we throw the baby out with the bath water and never receive the truth. Is the answer to let down our guard and relax our standards? No, this has never been an adequate solution. The correct approach is to be a willing student. We must apply ourselves to learning how to tell these two twins apart. Rejecting everything for fear of making a mistake can be too convenient. There may even be an element of laziness associated with it.

If we add spiritual pride to this attitude of laziness we end up justifying ourselves with thoughts like "I would rather err on the side of caution" or "I would rather be safe than sorry." It sounds spiritual and mature, but it may have roots of fear and an unwillingness to try. In these ways we reject God's voice of inward pictures.

The good news is that seeing inward pictures is easy! Start looking and you may be amazed at what you see!

9 Characteristics of Seeing

It was a once-in-a-lifetime experience. I was in Sunderland, England, for a conference and the evening before the conference began, arrangements were made for all the visiting ministers to have dinner in an old English castle. As we sat down to a scrumptious meal of roast brisket, I drank in the sights of the ancient building. I could almost see the ruler of the castle hosting a banquet for his lords and ladies.

What a great place for a romantic weekend with my wife. We could rent a room for the weekend, stroll the inner courtyards and enjoy the atmosphere of ancient England. As we toured the castle grounds after dinner, I tried to remember every detail to tell Mary later.

I arrived home in Florida, bursting with the good news of a romantic get-a-way in England, but soon discovered how difficult it was to describe. The castle was so much more exotic than anything I could describe with mere words. The sight of something five centuries old had a greater sense of history than its description.

Perhaps this is why God gave us five senses instead of one. Each one of our senses—seeing, hearing, taste, touch and smell—has their place. Seeing the castle was so much better than hearing about it. I had seen the castle, Mary was only hearing about it.

Seeing has many qualities that make it special among the senses. Let's explore some wonderful qualities of this God-given sense keeping in mind that these attributes apply to spiritual seeing as well.

A Picture is Worth a Thousand Words

The adage "a picture is worth a thousand words" is true of my experience in trying to describe the castle to Mary. I learned more about it in one minute of observing than she did in hours of explanation.

God created seeing as an efficient means of gathering information. I have often wondered how I would explain color to a blind person. How is blue different from red? One glance would be more meaningful than a library of books. When God wants to give us information quickly, He often uses pictures. He can provide us with vast amounts of information almost instantly by showing us a picture.

In my training courses I use the example of a sailboat. Suppose you are praying for someone and God shows you a sailboat on the water. As you ponder this image, it becomes clear that God wants the person to raise the sail of their faith to catch the wind of His Spirit. This will give them the strength to go on.

God uses visual images to communicate with us efficiently and effectively. He can convey the meaning to us more rapidly by using a picture than if He spoke to us in words.

God uses what we know

Just after getting married Mary and I moved into our first home. One of my first projects was to put in a grass yard. Before I started planting grass seed I did a good bit of research on the types of grass that thrive in our climate. I even had a sample of dirt from my yard tested by the University of Florida to detect nutrients, Ph values and other valuable information. I enjoy learning and researching new topics so this was a natural approach for me.

As a result I gained a fair amount of knowledge about grass. I learned that to have a healthy lawn free of weeds the grass needs three things: nutrients, water and mowing. If these are done properly then the grass will choke out the weeds.

The Lord used this to speak to me about parenting. He compared fertilizer with instruction, watering to affection, and mowing to discipline. He said if a child is provided with each of these in a healthy way, their spiritual growth would choke out the weeds of rebellion and sin. By building on my knowledge, God communicated a powerful truth to me about parenting in just seconds. It was as if it leapt into my mind fully developed.

In a similar way, God "spoke" to Peter in a trance on the house-top. God gave Peter the revelation to preach the gospel to the Gentiles through a vision of clean and unclean food. As a Jew, Peter observed the dietary laws of Moses so this was an area of knowledge for him. God used Peter's knowledge of clean and unclean food to tell Peter to include the "unclean" Gentiles in the church. We see this in other places in Scripture. Paul the tentmaker compared the church to a building. Jesus told Peter the fisherman that He would make him a fisher of men. Paul, the educated Pharisee, compared the law with our school master. Be prepared for God to speak to you through your knowledge and interests.

Understanding the setting and context of visions.

A Broadway play often has very elaborate sets. These backdrops literally "set the stage" for the action of the play. They provide context, location, and often they stimulate our senses with their beauty. A set doesn't exist for itself. It provides a place for the story. God-given pictures also have a setting. The setting of a picture from God doesn't exist for itself; it provides background for the primary elements.

To illustrate this better, let me ask you some questions about the sailboat we discussed earlier. Is the boat in the water, on a trailer, or somewhere else? Is the water calm or rough? Is it green, blue, or gray? Can you see land? What color is the boat? What color is the sail? Is the boat at anchor, adrift, or sailing? What time of day is it? What else do you see?

All of the details your answers provide may have no bearing on the message God wants to communicate. In our example, God said nothing of water, colors, or land. Yet when He puts a picture within us it often has these supporting details that provide context. Why does He give us details that have no meaning? The parables of Jesus give us a clue.

A parable is a short allegory or metaphor that uses a natural truth to communicate a spiritual truth. In the parable of the sower, Jesus said the sower sowed seeds on four types of ground: hard, shallow, thorny and good. The plants came to fruition only in the good soil—some thirty-fold, some sixty-fold, some one-hundred-fold.

There are only three primary elements in this parable: 1.) the seed is the gospel message; 2.) the soil is the heart of the hearer with the types of soil representing the condition of the heart; and, 3.) the birds represent Satan and his demons.

This is the full meaning of the parable. Yet there are many details left unexplained. Were the seeds wheat seeds or mustard seeds? Were the seeds watered by rain, irrigation or well water? Did the sower plant an entire field or just a few seeds dropped here and there? What is the meaning of the day of harvest? Jesus didn't address any of these questions.

A picture from God, like a parable, has only a few key elements that have meaning. Everything else is setting and has no purpose other than to support the meaningful elements. Then why is it given? Doesn't it just confuse matters to include elements in a picture that have no meaning? Not when we understand context. God includes these supportive elements because to omit them would be unnatural and confusing.

In our illustration of the sailboat it would be unnatural to see a sailboat hanging motionlessly on a white background as if the painter finished the boat and left the rest of the canvas blank. That's not how we see things in real life. God provides context because our soul requires it. Our mind may object to seeing a sailboat with no color on the boat or sail. This is particularly true when we factor in that God frequently speaks to us through our interests and knowledge.

Through my research on grass He spoke to me about parenting. The person most likely to hear from God in the form of a sailboat is someone familiar with sailing. When God shows a sailor a picture of a sailboat, his mind may object if the picture isn't accurate in all of its details. He may even be distracted by inaccuracies rather than focusing his attention on what is truly important.

For these reasons, God fills in the details as background and setting. The details have no spiritual meaning, but they must be present if the picture is to be compelling to the viewer. A further reason is that if the picture is accurate in all respects, the picture is likely to affect the viewer more strongly.

If I see a space shuttle launch as if I were right there, I am moved profoundly. If it is presented as a cartoon image, I am put off by it. The stronger that the image impacts the viewer, the more compelling is their recounting to the ultimate audience. This is important because if God is speaking to someone through us, we are more likely to convey it in a compelling way if we are moved by it.

The Meaning is Often Difficult to Determine

The viewer of the picture may have learned how to receive images from the Lord. Yet they may not have learned how to derive meaning from it. The depth and clarity of the pictures God gives to some people may amaze us. Yet they may disappoint us when we ask them what it means. Too often the answer is "I don't know" or "That's for you to figure out." Seeing is one thing, understanding is something else altogether.

A good way to understand the meaning of God-pictures is to start with the obvious. A common sense approach is often the most effective. We must avoid the temptation to over-spiritualize what we see. Keep your feet firmly on the ground when interpreting.

Another helpful practice is to seek advice from those who know you well and can be honest with you. We tend to avoid the unpleasant. We may not want to admit that we are stubborn, selfish or unstable. When God talks to us in pictures about these issues, we may want to understand them in a more favorable light. Having a good friend who can speak the truth in love is valuable.

Experience is perhaps the best teacher. The more we look for pictures and prayerfully seek their true meaning, the easier it will become. I remember when I first learned to drive. The controls on the car were difficult enough. Judging stopping distances was hard for me. I was confused by the different stripes on the road and what they meant. I was a nervous wreck before shifting out of park! With time it all became second nature. I graduated from an automatic to a stick shift and was downshifting to slow before I knew it. Now I drive without giving much thought to it.

Hearing from God is like this. At first it seems there is too much to know and you can't possibly remember it all. With experience you will be hearing almost effortlessly.

Start slowly. A new driver might do well to start in the parking lot and then move onto a straight stretch of country road before driving in city traffic. When learning to hear from God, start slowly. Before asking God who the next president will be or the identity of the Antichrist, you might want to begin with the missing sock from the dryer. I am notorious for putting things down where they don't belong. In the last few months I have begun asking the Lord where these misplaced items are and I am amazed how often He clearly shows me.

Stay with a few key elements. When viewing a God-picture, look for meaning among the most prominent points. Don't try to derive too much meaning from the picture and don't try to derive meaning from every element of the picture. Usually the Lord wants to point

out a few basic points. In our excitement we may look at every detail
of the picture for meaning and think we have found it. I caution
against this for those starting on their journey of hearing from God.
It is very easy for our soul to fill in the missing meaning, leaving us
with an incorrect understanding. Keep it simple and clear.

The Lord frequently uses symbolic language. He may use one
thing to represent something else, which is known as a 'type'. Manna,
the bread from heaven given to the Israelites in the wilderness, is a
type of Christ (John 6:32-35). Types, shadows, parables and some
Old Testament prophecy are all examples of symbolic language.

God also speaks clearly and literally. We find both types of communication in John 11:11 surrounding the death of Lazarus. Jesus
says Lazarus is sleeping and that He is going to Bethany to wake him
up. Verse 13 tells us this was symbolic language for the death of
Lazarus and Jesus raising him from the dead. However, the disciples
interpreted it literally by responding that if he is sick and sleeping, it
will help him get better.

In verse 14 Jesus tells them plainly "Lazarus is dead." Jesus used
both literal and symbolic language. In Mark 4 He speaks in the symbolic language of parables, and then tells the disciples in private the
literal meaning of the parable.

Symbols and their meanings

Some symbols have an absolute meaning assigned by God that
doesn't vary. Other symbols may mean one thing to one person and
something different to another. When God speaks to us in symbolic
language, it helps to understand which symbols God has already
assigned a meaning to and which He has not.

For example, the word "anoint" means to smear with oil. Oil is a
symbol of the Holy Spirit and anointing, and abundance[28]. If you
have seen a God-picture that contains oil, its likely interpretation
relates to the person and work of the Holy Spirit. Seas, according to
Unger's Bible Dictionary, are a symbol of the seething nations of the
world and of the troubled lives of the unrighteous (Dan. 7:2-3; Matt.
13:47; Rev. 13:1).

The meanings of most symbols are not defined in Scripture and are
subject to interpretation. The Lord has shown me footballs, cars,
houses, and countless other symbols that may mean one thing to me
and another thing to someone else. They may mean one thing in one
picture the Lord is showing me and something different in another
picture He gives me.

How do we know which objects have meaning and which are context and do not? Of those things that do have meaning, how do we know what meaning it has in this picture and what meaning it may have in another picture? Searching the Scriptures will help you learn the things to which the Lord has already assigned meaning. A reputable book on symbols is helpful. Be careful you don't choose a resource that takes signs and symbols to an extreme. Experience and a pure heart are your best tools for interpreting symbols that have a subjective meaning. Ask God to show you their meaning as it changes from case to case.

A Word of Caution. Symbolic language captures the imagination and opens the possibilities for depth of meaning that literal speech does not. Some people have a tendency to derive greater meaning from a God-picture than the Lord intends. This is exacerbated when they are genuinely hungry for more of God. They are on a quest and may find more than He is revealing. Those who enjoy metaphorical language can also make the mistake of taking it further than God intends.

The Exception is a Small Group Known as Seers. For every general rule there is an exception. The general rule is that a God-picture contains a limited number of key truths. The remainder of the picture provides setting and context. The exception is found in the Old Testament as a type of prophet known as a seer. The Lord spoke to seers in prophetic visions that contained a great deal of detail.

The book of Ezekiel contains many prophetic visions and symbolic images. The book of Revelation is also very symbolic and contains a staggering amount of depth and detail. We must make room for the fact that God will speak to some people using a great amount of symbolism. The images He shows them may have a tremendous amount of detail and information. In its proper place this is an effective and powerful means of communication.

The Condition of The Heart

When God does something significant in our life that is so powerful it changes our course, we may have a tendency to venerate the experience. God gave Jacob a dream where he saw angels ascending and descending to earth on a ladder. In the dream God reaffirmed His covenant with Abraham and extended it to Jacob. Jacob's response was that the land was holy and the place he was laying was a gateway to heaven. He made a pillar of rocks he used for pillows and poured oil over them in testimony of what God had shown him.

Similarly we may remember the lodge where God ministered to us during a retreat, or the little church where we accepted Jesus as Savior. We may find ourselves venerating an experience or place rather than keeping our focus clearly on the Lord. When God shows us a picture, it may move us deeply. It may cause us to surrender more completely to Him or it may be a powerful way to minister to someone. When we have a strong spiritual experience, we must be careful not to focus on the dream, picture, vision or other form of communication.

It isn't the dream or picture that is important—it is God and what He is saying that is important. If we forget this, we may find ourselves making an idol of a dream or a vision. We may make it more significant in our life than God intended.

An Issue of Personal Value

God created people with a strong need for personal value. A person who is spiritually and mentally healthy feels good about who they are. The Lord intends for us to derive our sense of value directly from Him. It is His love for us, the price He paid for us on Calvary, and who He has destined us to be that gives us value. When we try to derive a sense of value from the opinions of others, we become people-pleasers doing what we think will curry favor with others. When we get value from our work, we feel good about ourselves because of what we have done, not who we are. This results in a need to perform to feel valuable.

These are unhealthy ways to gain a sense of value, importance and significance. The person who is not receiving their sense of value from God is vulnerable to the deception of getting value from their spiritual experiences.

For this kind of value to be compelling, it must elevate the person above others and reinforces that they are precious and unique. The lie supporting this deception sounds something like this: "Because I have visions that are more detailed and specific than anyone else, I am special to God and therefore very valuable."

Ultimately this can lead to the exclusivism of a cult leader (or a member) who proclaims that he or she alone has the true gospel and everyone else is wrong. New members must accept the "truth" of the leader's teaching in order to be saved.

The sincere Christian is at very little risk of taking things to this extreme. However, it is possible that without a healthy sense of value from the Lord they will put a wrong emphasis on what God has shown them.

Some Christians aren't satisfied in their pursuit of the Lord. Others have a low sense of value. The Christian with both may want to derive greater meaning from what he sees. He may want to use these experiences to prove that he is spiritual and therefore valuable. This may result in an otherwise good person flaunting his spiritual experiences in front of others to lift himself up. This leads to horror stories about what people do if released to hear the voice of God. It becomes easier for pastors to stifle people than it is to deal with these issues.

Seeing is a wonderful means of communication that is efficient and powerful. However, it can be misused. Let's recognized the benefits of this 'language' and avoid the abuses.

10 God's Inner Voice

I had finished my sermon at a church near St. Louis, Missouri, and was now ministering to people who had come forward for prayer. I looked over to a group of about five or six people sitting together when I heard a voice say, "Angela." It wasn't an audible voice, but an inner whisper. I was excited that God had given me a name even though He didn't say anything more.

Not knowing who Angela was or what I should do, I decided to take a step of faith. Since I was looking at this group of people when I heard the name, I thought perhaps it related to one of them. I walked over and told them what was happening. I asked if one of them was named Angela. The look on their faces was a pleasant, but a flat "no."

I had already gone public with the name so I figured it would do no harm to see if I could discern what God was saying. I asked if any of them was concerned about or praying for an Angela. Again "no." Did any of them know an Angela? "No." This was going nowhere— I was tempted to ask if anyone had ever heard the name Angela! Yet with each question, I had a growing conviction that the whispered name inside me was coming from God. In fact, the whispering voice was now giving me details. I felt Angela was a young woman in her early teens who desperately needed God's help and protection. Finally I turned from the small group and appealed to the whole congregation. The familiar "no" answered me.

By this time, I was convinced God was speaking and we needed to pray for Angela even though no one knew her. There was an arising

faith among the people—God already had met with us and ministered in powerful ways. Inside I was a bit shaken by how this was
turning out. Nevertheless, we prayed. I prayed for God to put a
hedge of protection around Angela like He did Job. I prayed God
would protect her wherever she was and that He would intervene and
take care of her. The congregation responded in faith with a spirited
"Amen!"

At breakfast the next morning the pastor confessed he didn't know
anything about "Angela" either. He was kind, but seemed unsure
whether God was involved. I thought little more about it until weeks
later when a pastor friend, who had been at that service, came to our
city for a conference.

"Did you hear about Angela?" he asked excitedly. "No, I haven't,"
I answered, inwardly cringing at the mention of the name. He told
me a remarkable story about a fourteen-year-old girl named Angela
who had turned state's evidence on a prostitution ring in which she
was involved. Twelve people were jailed!

Not only that, but Angela's school teacher was among the five people to whom I was originally drawn. I remembered how we prayed
for Angela and asked God to protect her and watch over her during
this critical time. It stunned me to realize that we had prayed so accurately in faith for this young woman, using her very name. God's gentle voice led us as His instruments for Angela. It is humbling and
amazing to realize that by simple obedience any of us have the privilege of powerfully affecting a person's life for God.

God's Inner Voice

Earlier we looked at 1 Kings 19 and how it describes the inner
voice of the Lord as a "still small voice." It is a delicate, whispering
voice inside us and an identical twin to the voice of our heart. At first,
we often confuse these two twins. This is why we ask ourselves "Is
this me or God?" We are listening to twin voices and we can't tell
them apart. We don't know if what we are hearing is coming from
God or from our heart.

If we know one twin, we can get an idea of what the other looks
like even if we have never seen him (or her). The twin we know is the
voice of our heart. We know what it is like to talk to ourselves. We
have been listening to this inner voice all of our life. We are so familiar with it that we might fail to realize that we hear it. Try this fun
exercise to refresh your memory about the inner voice of your heart.

Exercise:

1.) Say your first and last name in your mind without making any sound with your voice. Did you hear a voice? Did it sound the same as talking to yourself? Now try a variation on this.
2.) Say your first and last name in your mind without making any sound with your voice. This time whisper (not with your voice, but in your mind). Could you tell a difference? Try one last variation.
3.) Say your first and last name in your mind without making any sound with your voice. This time SHOUT (not with your voice, but in your mind). Big difference, eh?

Many characteristics of the inner voice of our heart are identical to the inner voice of the Lord. Before we explore how much alike they are, it is important we clearly understand that these two voices are different. They sound alike, but they are very different.

When I heard the name Angela, it was like it popped into my mind out of nowhere. It felt no different from any other thought or impression. I could have easily dismissed it as just me. Yet because it happened during a time of ministry when I was expecting the Lord to speak, I was careful not to reject it.

Same Language, Different Speaker

In Chapter 2 we discussed the languages God gave us when He created mankind. One of these is an inner voice. When we use this voice, we are "talking to ourselves." When God uses this voice, it is God talking to us. The language and sound doesn't change, but the speaker does. Because it is the same language, it sounds the same regardless who is speaking.

Oh, how often we have rejected God's voice because it sounded like our heart! This is perhaps the greatest single reason for not hearing the voice of the Lord.

During our engagement, Mary lived in Orlando and I lived eight hours away in Florida's Panhandle area where the ministry I work for is located. One day Mary called the ministry and Scott, my brother, answered the phone. Because Scott and I sound so much alike she thought it was me. We sound alike, but are very different.

How can we learn to hear God's voice with clarity, consistency and confidence? The first step is to listen for an inner voice that sounds much like the inner voice of our heart. Remember the imposters from Chapter 6: the wind, the earthquake and the fire? Don't listen for a mysterious voice, a powerful voice, or a judgmental voice. Be sensitive to the small, quiet voice just like your heart.

There are many examples of the inner voice of the Lord in Scripture. In Chapter 3 we discussed how Samuel heard it as a young boy (1 Sam. 3:2-5). Jesus told us that the Holy Spirit will speak to us in this way:[30]

> What I tell you in the dark, speak in the daylight; what is whispered in your ear, proclaim from the roofs (Matt. 10:27).

The Psalmist refers to this inner voice in Psalm 85:8, speaking peace:

> I will listen to what God the LORD will say; he promises peace to his people, his saints–but let them not return to folly.

Elijah heard it on the mountain when God told him to anoint kings[31]. This is one of the most prolific ways God speaks!

Easy to Hear, Hard to Believe

Hearing the inner voice of the Lord is one of the easiest things we will ever do! It is easier than grocery shopping, parenting, manual labor, and surrendering our life to Christ. In fact, there is nothing difficult about hearing God's inner voice. It is a whispering voice within us that comes to us frequently and unbidden. It leaps up within us when we aren't listening for it. How often have we heard the Lord call us to prayer? How often have we heard Him talk to us about our attitudes, thoughts and our life?

God's inner voice is easy to hear, but it may be hard to believe! He often speaks to us, but we may rarely believe that it is His voice. We seem prone to disbelief. We may acknowledge that it is Him when we are in the safety of our home. Or when nothing is at stake and we don't need to take action. Yet when there is a risk of error, we may respond with a fear of failure or fear of making a mistake. Our confidence evaporates.

What a wonderful life it would be if we could not only hear God's inner voice, but believe everything He says to us. Imagine the possibilities if we had a continual conversation with the Lord! Consider the light in our lives if we could talk not just to Him, but with Him at anytime!

Nothing is stopping us. Let's listen to His voice within us and believe what He says.

11 God's Audible Voice

My cousin had my full attention. "I was standing right here by my closet," he said, "when I heard God's audible voice." He said it sounded like it was coming from right behind him. I never heard God speak this way and was intrigued. Plus, it had happened to someone I knew. Maybe if I stayed long enough I would hear it too!

Mark continued his story. He had been getting ready that morning to go job hunting. As he was getting clothes out of his closet, he heard God's audible voice telling him where to apply. He was obedient and got the job.

The audible voice of the Lord is what we hear with our physical ears just as we hear the voices of people. Hearing God's audible voice is more rare than hearing His inner voice. Yet many people have heard God speak aloud. When I conduct seminars on hearing God's voice, I often ask how many attending have heard God speak in an audible voice. Usually between twenty to fifty percent of the audience raise their hand. At first this high number amazed me, perhaps because I had never heard God speak in this way. But the numbers have remained consistently high over the years, so I am adjusting my beliefs about how often God speaks in this way.

In the Bible, we often find that this voice seems to come from behind the hearer.[32] Whether there is any meaning or significance to this is difficult to say. Of those in the seminars who have heard God speak aloud, the majority concur that it sounded as if it came from behind. However, this is not the universal experience.

Why an Audible Voice?

A supernatural manifestation of this magnitude is certainly not an everyday event. Why does the Lord use it so rarely and for what special occasions does He reserve it? From an examination of Scripture, it does not appear that God uses this obviously miraculous voice to inspire faith in the hearer. In fact, He may not use it for the benefit of the one to whom He is speaking, but for others. When He spoke to Jesus just prior to His crucifixion (John 12:28), Jesus said that the voice was for the sake of those who also heard it.

God spoke to Moses audibly so the Israelites would believe Moses (Ex. 19:9). This suggests that God may speak in an audible voice not for the one being spoken to, but for the others who also hear it.

God seems to reserve His audible voice for times of special significance: the baptism of Jesus, Daniel receiving divine revelation about the ages to come, the transfiguration of Jesus, the conversion of Paul, Peter being told that the gospel was for Gentiles, and Job's confrontation with God as He spoke from the whirlwind. God reserves His audible voice for times of great importance and for emphasizing the magnitude of the message.

As one who has never heard God's audible voice, I find it difficult to understand why anyone would doubt it. It seems faith would be automatic. Interestingly, those who question this voice often questioned His inner voice. Hebrews 11:6 says that "without faith it is impossible to please God." His audible voice still requires faith to believe. He doesn't speak in this way to remove the need for us to believe by faith.

On occasions, those hearing God's audible voice were not convinced, even by this powerful sign from heaven. A case in point is the Apostle Paul's experience on the Damascus road. Paul's traveling companions saw the light, were knocked to the ground, and heard God's voice[33]. Yet the Bible never mentions them as converted or responding in faith in any way. We never again hear about any of these men. Paul alone believed:

> *"So then, King Agrippa, I was not disobedient to the vision from heaven. First to those in Damascus, then to those in Jerusalem and in all Judea, and to the Gentiles also, I preached that they should repent and turn to God and prove their repentance by their deeds (Acts 26:19-20).*

We see this lack of faith in those surrounding Jesus. As He neared His death, the Father spoke audibly to Him[34]. Jesus said it was for those who stood by, yet their reaction was not one of faith. Some said it thundered, others said an angel spoke to Him. Yet no one said it was God speaking. No one seemed to believe that God the Father was speaking to God the Son. Though Jesus said God intended the voice for them, it didn't seem to have any affect on them, certainly not compelling them to believe. Neither with Paul nor with Jesus did those who heard the voice respond in faith. This suggests that whether God's voice is audible, or whether He speaks in a still, small voice within us, it requires faith to believe.

God still speaks in an audible voice today. If you are blessed to hear Him in this way, you may find it takes faith to believe just as it does to believe His inner voice. You may also find that God has reserved this special way of communicating for this very significant time in your life!

12 Characteristics of Hearing

Each method of communication has purposes for which it is well-suited and other purposes for which it is not. For example, the visual language of pictures is good for communicating a large amount of information quickly, but it can be poor at conveying meaning. On the other hand, hearing is poor for conveying large amounts of information, but is good for developing relationships.

Hearing has its own characteristics, some are good and some are not as good. In this chapter we will explore these attributes and learn how to benefit from God's wonderful method of communicating by hearing.

Easy to Convey

Repeating a message verbatim is an easy way to communicate exactly what we have heard. This guarantees that we deliver the message just as we received it. At my home sometimes a message from Mom or Dad gets passed from child to child. As long as each person repeats the precise wording of the message, the last person hears the original message.

The principle of exact duplication has insured the accuracy of the Bible we have today. Scribes and those entrusted with copying the Bible in ancient times employed elaborate measures to ensure they made no errors when penning a fresh copy of the Scriptures. To ensure they didn't misplace a single word, they counted to the middle word of the book being copied. It had to match the original exactly. If the copy passed this test, they performed a more exact one by counting to the middle letter of the document.

These, and other demanding practices, guaranteed that the copy was identical to the original. Over the centuries this method has proven its value. In 1947 a shepherd boy made an important archaeological discovery of ancient copies of the Old Testament known as the Dead Sea Scrolls. These writings were made between 250 B.C. and 68 A.D.[35] When we compare these ancient writings with the Bible, we find them in agreement. This assures us that we have the same Scriptures that Jesus did and validates the method of repeating word-for-word to insure the integrity of the message.

When Mary and I first got married, the Lord said to me, "Treat your wife like a queen." Occasionally I convey this message to other young married men by simply repeating the words God said to me. I give the message to them precisely as God gave it to me. The other day Mary and I were in the car and in a playful mood. I said to her, "If I treat you like a queen that makes me a..." I let my words hang in the air, waiting for her to tell me I was her king. Instead, she said "...my servant!"

Even when the meaning of the message is unknown, verbatim repetition can preserve it. Bible translators are careful to translate exactly what God's Word says from one language to another. They preserve its wording even when they have differing opinions as to its meaning. A case in point is the phrase "Climb Mount Nitaka," which was the code phrase used for commencing the Japanese attack on Pearl Harbor. This message could accurately pass through the Japanese chain of command even if the intermediaries didn't understand its meaning.

When the Lord speaks to us, the precise wording is often important. With people, on the other hand, what they say is less important than the meaning they intend to convey. We often misuse language and grope for words, assuming others will read between the lines to discern our true meaning. However, God uses the right words, making the precise wording important.

Repeating the message just as we have heard it doesn't always assure the meaning is clear. When we hear the word "doe," do we understand it to mean a female deer, uncooked bread, slang for money or a musical note? We can easily repeat the words, but we may not be able to convey the meaning.

This may be a drawback, but it also can be a benefit. A private message can be cryptically spoken in public while only those who know "the code" understand the hidden meaning. My kids know that when in public I say, "Would you like a taco?", I am really telling them that they are misbehaving and are on the verge of discipline. Of course, this becomes a problem at Taco Bell©. How odd that they prefer Wendy's©!

Limited Information

If a picture is worth a thousand words, then it follows that it takes a thousand words to describe a picture. Words are relatively inefficient at communicating large amounts of information. We can identify a stranger more easily by seeing a picture of them than by hearing a description of them.

Words are inadequate when conveying moving experiences or deep emotions. The victim of a tragedy may say to their counselor, "You don't know how I feel unless it has happened to you." Hearing their description of the event doesn't have the same impact as experiencing it personally.

Conversely, words can be more definite and precise than either pictures or feelings. Examples of this are the language used in legal contracts, technical manuals and laws.

The combination of these two qualities means that when the message is short but specific, words are a good choice for communicating.

Requires Nearness

We must be near the source of a sound to hear it clearly. This is particularly true with the Lord because He often speaks with a soft voice. This means we must have a close relationship with Him if we are to hear His voice clearly. The closer a marriage is, the better the husband and wife hear the true meaning of each other's words.

This concerns the chain of events that occur with hearing. A message from the heart must first be spoken with the mouth, then heard with the ears, and finally interpreted with the heart. This chain of heart-mouth-ears-heart is only half of the communication. The hearer then interprets the message, not as the speaker's heart expressed it, but in the way the hearer's heart heard it. Their response then goes from their heart-to mouth-to ears-to heart, where it is again interpreted. This process has great potential for misunderstanding. The better the hearer knows the speaker and understands their heart, the more accurately they interpret the speaker's heartfelt meaning.

The degree to which we know the Lord and are walking intimately with Him is the degree to which we will accurately interpret what He is saying to us.

Drowned Out

My son was walking out of his classroom at school one day and passed by a large, noisy air conditioner. He saw our car in the parking lot and called out to me. I was far enough away that I could clearly hear Jonathan's voice over the noise. Standing next to the noise, he couldn't hear my shouted greeting in return. His voice was clear to me, but mine was drowned out to him.

Noise created by fear, confusion and reason can drown out the voice of the Lord. He hears us, but we may not hear Him. When in this situation, we may feel inundated or overwhelmed. We cry out to God asking for help. Yet when He answers us and speaks peace and comfort, we may not hear it. We are left feeling alone, unaided, perhaps even abandoned by God in our hour of need.

God has made a wonderful provision for us in these situations. The sound of what is truly important can cut through the din, allowing His message to reach us. (For more clarity, review Chapter 3, "A Matter of Value, Not Volume.")

Hearing and Relationships

Verbal communication is essential for building strong relationships. The adoring look of a husband may say, "I love you!" to his wife. However, if he wants her to know all of the reasons he loves her, he must talk.

Consider how difficult it would be if a husband and wife didn't speak the same language. Their actions and gestures may communicate love, even dedication, but without verbal communication the relationship would be severely limited. Words can communicate more specifically than either vision or feeling.

Hearing has many wonderful qualities that make it ideal for communicating under certain conditions, but it is also limited. When we recognize both its assets and liabilities, we have a greater appreciation for this means of communicating.

13 Inner Witness

The judge was presiding over a trial that might result in the death penalty. As he listened to the prosecution's case, a perfumed letter arrived from his wife that he discreetly opened and read to himself. She pleaded with him to set the accused free. She wrote how she had dreamed about this man. The dream moved her so deeply that she was convinced the man was innocent.

The judge was Pontius Pilate, described as "an unprincipled achiever who was willing to sacrifice what was right to accomplish his own selfish goals[36]. We don't know if his wife, Claudia Procula, was embarrassed that she had dreamed about another man nor do we know if it took courage for her to intervene.

What we do know is that the dream convinced her of Jesus' innocence and she tried to spare His life.

While Pilate was sitting on the judge's seat, his wife sent him this message: "Don't have anything to do with that innocent man, for I have suffered a great deal today in a dream because of him" (Matt. 27:19).

Although Pontius Pilate recognized Jesus' innocence and had the authority to uphold justice and acquit Him, he gave into the demands of the crowd. He refused his wife's request and turned Jesus over for the Jews to crucify rather than risk a personal setback in his career[37].

The feelings that Claudia Procula experienced that night are translated as "suffered" in Matthew 27:19. The Greek word is pascho, which means to experience a sensation or impression (usually painful). While we normally understand it as negative or painful, it also means simply "to feel" as in Acts 28:5 when a snake bit Paul:

And he shook off the beast into the fire, and felt no harm [pascho].

Pilate's wife experienced a sensation or impression during her dream that convinced her of Jesus' innocence. Some dreams are more compelling than others, some take the better part of a day to shake off. Apparently this dream moved Claudia so deeply that she attempted to interfere with the judicial process by sending a written appeal to her husband.

God can speak through feelings and impressions. It is possible that God gave Claudia Procula a dream to cause her to believe strongly in Jesus' innocence. Because of these feelings, she dared to approach her husband.

God used feelings to communicate with Jesus. The Bible teaches us that Jesus didn't act according to His own will, but only did what the Father led Him to do. In John 5:19 we see the Father leading Jesus in a visual way:

Then Jesus answered and said to them, "Most assuredly, I say to you, the Son can do nothing of Himself, but what He sees the Father do; for whatever He does, the Son also does in like manner (John 5:19).

In verse 30 we find the Father leading Jesus in a hearing way:

By myself I can do nothing; I judge only as I hear, and my judgment is just, for I seek not to please myself but him who sent me (John 5:30).

In Matthew 14:14 Jesus is lead by a sensation or impression. This was another manner in which the Father communicated with His Son:

When Jesus landed and saw a large crowd, he had compassion on them and healed their sick.

We know that Jesus was not acting according to His own will or desire when He healed the people. He did only those things that pleased His Father[38]:

The one who sent me is with me; he has not left me alone, for I always do what pleases him (John 8:29).

In Matthew 14:14, Jesus perceived the will of the Father based on how He felt. He interpreted the feeling of compassion as the will of God and was obedient to the Father's leading by healing the multitude.

God also speaks to us through sensations and leads us by feeling. How often have we been spared harm because we had a feeling of foreboding and changed our plans? How often have we made gut-level decisions that turned out to be God? How we "feel" can be the Lord speaking to us. When we learn to honor this voice, we become much more perceptive to His leading.

Romans 8:16 refers to this agreement between how we feel and the will of God as "bearing witness."

The Spirit Himself bears witness with our spirit that we are children of God. (NKJ)

We also may call this "a witness of the spirit." In either case the idea is the same. The word translated as "witness" in Romans 8:16 is summartureo, which means two or more witnesses jointly, yet distinctly, giving testimony to the same fact. Two witnesses are mentioned here: the spirit of the man himself and the Spirit of God.[39] "The testimony of the Spirit is an inward impression on the souls of believers."[40] Our spirit expresses its agreement with God through a feeling or an impression. We call God-given feelings an "inner witness."

Conscience is the Twin

God may use feelings to speak to us just as He did with Jesus. The twin to this voice is our conscience. It too speaks with feelings. When we contemplate an action that we believe is morally wrong, our conscience responds with feelings of anxiety, unsettledness or foreboding.

The New Unger's Bible Dictionary describes the conscience as "An exercise of the judgment and the power of feeling"[41]. This highlights two important factors of the twin. First, Unger's mentions "an exercise of the judgment." This specifically identifies this voice as coming from our own values, reason and morals, not from God.

Second, Unger's refers to "the power of feeling." We might understand this as the way in which the conscience makes its displeasure known. It doesn't speak to us in words or show us pictures. It causes us to feel. These feelings can range from mildly uncomfortable to deeply troubling. Noted Christian author James Stalker, in his article on the punitive conscience, says:

In the individual's own breast are not only the figures of justice already mentioned, but the executioner as well; for, on the back of a sentence of condemnation or acquittal, there immediately follows the pain of a wounded or the satisfaction of an approving conscience; and of all human miseries or blisses this is the most poignant.[42]

The powerful imagery employed by Stalker rings true to those who have been vexed by their conscience.

Discerning between the inner witness of the Lord and our feelings requires great maturity. Feelings are powerful and we tend to protect them. We may insist they are from God and we shouldn't change them. Interestingly, it has been my experience that when a person hears something, they are reluctant to believe it is from God ("It's just me"). Yet when they feel, they are likely to think it is God ("My spirit doesn't bear witness to that.").

Important Caution

Two factors may make our feelings a poor way of determining what God is saying. First, we tend to believe what we feel comes from God. Second, we resist changing how we feel. When these two join, our attitude may be "I believe what I feel is from God and I'm unwilling to change."

The danger is that we may hear from our heart, but believe it is from the Lord. Our response is to resist any change in feelings. We can become entrenched in what we believe, thinking it is from God, when it is really from us.

We can avoid this in several ways. First, we can surrender what we feel to the Lord. Rather than insisting we have heard from God, we can continually surrender our feelings to Him. We can continue to feel without needing to defend our feelings.

Second, we can ask for confirmation. God will use other sources to either validate that what we are feeling is from Him, or show us that they are not. The Bible encourages us to seek confirmation:

Every matter must be established by the testimony of two or three witnesses (2 Cor. 13:1, see also Matt.18:16).

For lack of guidance a nation falls, but many advisers make victory sure (Prov. 11:14).

When we ask advice of spiritual people, God can use them to affirm or correct what we think He is saying to us through our feelings.

Third, we can spend quality time in the presence of the Lord and let Him change us into His image. The more we are like Jesus, the less our feelings will lead us astray. They, too, will be like Jesus and there will be agreement between our feelings and the inner witness.

When we become aware of these dangers and respond correctly, we will be good stewards of this wonderful language of feeling. We also can then accurately hear from God through our feelings.

14 Knowing

As I sat nervously before the government official, I thought back to my junior year in high school when I had accepted Jesus as Savior. Almost immediately I had sensed a call to the ministry and began planning to attend Bible college. A year later, as high school graduation drew closer, I sensed I was supposed to postpone Bible college for a year.

This would be difficult because I was receiving financial aid from the government. As I kept praying about my future, I felt God directing me to attend a community college for a year. This would allow me to continue to receive assistance, while waiting to enroll in Bible college the following year.

All went well until I finished my year of community college and moved from Phoenix to San Antonio to attend Bible college. The federal agency providing my benefits requested an interview in their offices. They explained that in order for me to continue to receive assistance, they had to approve my change of major from "undeclared" to "theology." I thought they probably wanted to protect their investment and make sure I wasn't bouncing from school to school just to receive money.

They ended up scheduling me for several hours of exams, including aptitude, intelligence and interest tests. Finally, I sat down with a government official to go over my results. He pointed out that I had a strong interest in chemical engineering and my test scores supported my ability to pursue a career in that field. In a formal but fatherly way, he counseled me to pursue a career path in which I had strong interest and ability. He also suggested several other fields for my consideration.

As a young man far from home with no family or advisors, I was on my own. I was apprehensive facing this man who had a say on whether or not I would continue receiving financial aid. The mere fact that I was in a U.S. government office at his request was intimidating enough, but with no one to support me, I felt unsure of myself. However, I was convinced of one thing: God had called me to this Bible college to prepare me for my life's work in the ministry.

I decided to be honest and speak from my heart. I explained to the man that God had called me to the ministry and had directed me to this college a thousand miles from my home. As I spoke, I watched for a reaction. I had no idea what his religious background was or if he considered me a certifiable nut for believing God was talking to me.

He showed no reaction and proceeded to renew his position that I should pursue engineering or something else for which I was well-suited. I showed him the respect of genuinely considering his advice. I thought about the fields he was recommending. The tests were right. I did have a strong interest in those areas and felt I could fare well in any of these fields. School was never much of a problem for me. Yet I knew God had called me to the ministry. I remembered the night when I sensed it so strong. It was a definite feeling that almost overwhelmed me. It wasn't that I heard God say anything to me, and I hadn't seen an angel or a vision. It started as a feeling, but became a strong and growing conviction that I pondered for two years. I knew this was the right thing to do.

We were getting nowhere. This man was kind, but insistent. I told him God called me to the ministry and my personal interests and abilities didn't matter. What really mattered was the will of God and His purpose for my life and that I must obey. I told him that I was not willing to consider anything other than this college and this major. I politely stood my ground, praying under my breath that God would intervene and soften this man's heart.

Suddenly his face changed. He shuffled a few papers, put his stamp of approval on my form and sent me on my way. I never again had a bit of trouble from this agency.

"Knowing" Defined

There are times when we Christians have a strong sense of the will of God, but have nothing to prove our conviction. When asked how we know, sometimes the only answer is "I just know!" We can't explain it, defend it or prove it—we simply have a strong, undeniable belief. We may not even be able to explain why we feel as we do. There is often simply nothing to point to justifying why we feel the way we do. In an attempt to explain our feeling we use phrases like "I know that I know that I know" and "I know it in my knower!".

Characteristics of Knowing

Sometimes the Lord speaks to us by putting a strong feeling within us. We"know" what we should do. When this happens, we have an inner sense of certainty and confidence. Not only do we "know," but we feel confident about what we know. This certainty may be so strong that no amount of persuasion can talk us out of it. It stands in the face of opposition, logic and reason.

A Special Class of Inner Witness

In the previous chapter we discussed the voice of the Lord as an inner witness. We defined this as God speaking to us by causing us to feel a certain way. "Knowing" is this inner witness that also has confidence, boldness, even stubbornness associated with it. It is not different from the inner witness, but it is a special type of inner witness.

Examples of Knowing

In the Old Testament Abraham heard God tell him to leave his home in Ur by the Persian Gulf and head for present-day Israel. How did he know it was God who told him to do this? His father Terah worshiped other gods[43] and some have speculated that he was an idol maker[44]. Abraham couldn't have taken advice from him. What shored up his belief that this voice was from the Lord?

Another case in point is how Abraham knew that the covenant of circumcision was from God. The pagan religions in the area cut themselves to show dedication to their false god's[45]. How was Abraham to know it was God and not his cultural moorings speaking to him? Could it be that Abraham was a "knower" and that God spoke to him in a feeling way that resulted in strong beliefs and convictions?

Transcendence of Knowing

Knowing transcends circumstances, knowledge and personality. It goes beyond us. A woman in the Old Testament had enough food for one last meal for herself and her son. She was going to cook it, eat it and then prepare to die (1 Kin. 17). God's prophet told her to give him the meal. If she would obey, she would have enough to eat until the rain came and ended the famine. In spite of her circumstances, she believed God. When God causes us to "know," it doesn't matter if it contradicts our circumstances. The confidence and boldness that results overcomes any clash with surrounding conditions.

"Knowing" as a feeling is also independent of our knowledge of facts. Our head may contain knowledge that disagrees with the "knowing" in our spirit. This may result in a duality in the way we feel. On the one hand, we are aware of our normal thoughts and feelings concerning the matter. On the other hand, we have a strong "knowing" in our spirit. Because of the confidence and certainty that accompany "knowing," it can stand even when it conflicts with what we know.

"Knowing" is not based on our personality. Some people are strong-willed and feel passionately about everything. We might expect this personality type to know-that-they-know-that-they-know. However, when God speaks in a "knowing" way, even a meek person will respond with boldness. It isn't based on us—it is from Him.

"Knowing" is a powerful means of communication. It can be a compelling way for God to communicate with us. We may also abuse and misuse it. It has great potential for harm or for hurt. Therefore, we must handle it with the utmost maturity. In the next chapter, we will cover some of the strengths and weaknesses of this wonderful gift to help us use it in a manner pleasing to the Lord.

15 Characteristics of Feeling

The language of feeling, expressed as an inner witness, has its own unique set of characteristics. Some of these qualities make "feeling" a good method for communicating while some of its other qualities do not. By exploring the assets and liabilities of feeling, we can learn what it is best for and maximize its usefulness.

Feelings Motivate

Of the three types of languages (seeing, feeling and hearing), feeling moves us to action most. We might hear stories or see pictures about the plight of starving children in a foreign land and fail to do anything. However, when we feel love and compassion for them, our feelings move us to action. We must do something. This is because God made our feelings to be closely associated with our will.

This characteristic is beneficial in many respects. When we have revelation of the suffering of hell, it moves us to evangelism. When we feel the pain of a person who has had a tragic life, we look for a way to bring them healing and help. When Jesus saw the sick, He was moved with compassion (feeling) and healed them (action)[46].

The reciprocal of this is also true. When we share a common experience with others (action), we have much more compassion for them (feeling) though they may be different from us in every other way. Surviving a natural disaster together can unite total strangers. Sharing a foxhole in war can make lifelong friends of the rich and the poor, the simple and the wise, the common and the refined.

The principle of common experience affecting our feelings is a Scriptural one. The Living Bible relays it clearly in Hebrews 4:15 (brackets mine):

This High Priest of ours [Jesus] understands our weaknesses [compassion] since he had the same temptations we do [experiences], though he never once gave way to them and sinned.

The liability of this language is when we feel negative emotions and they motivate us to ungodly behavior. Lust and impulse buying are two examples of acting out of feelings rather than being motivated by truth and righteousness.

Another liability is becoming dependent upon feeling before we act. We might refuse to pray until we "feel like it." We may find ourselves doing what we "want" rather than what is right. Without the guiding principles of truth, and without discipline to keep feelings in their rightful place, they can be negative factors in our lives.

Feelings "Are Us"

When we see or hear, we may think of it as outside ourselves. Yet when we feel, it is part of us. We might say, "I had a thought," phrasing it as something that comes to us but is separate from us. With feelings we are more likely to say, "I feel this way." We think of feelings as part of us. This is because we have a sense of ownership of feelings. They are not something "out there." They are in us. They are us.

Because we identify our feelings with who we are, to deny them is to deny ourselves. When someone questions how we feel or says it is wrong, we might react defensively. It may feel like they have attacked us personally. We instinctively want to defend and justify our feelings.

The ultimate defense of our feelings is to believe that what we feel is from God. After all, if God has made us to feel this way, then who can call it into question? With no higher authority than God, who has the authority to challenge us?

This may result in "feeling-based" beliefs, which are dangerous and can lead to deception. The world manipulates through feelings, often with total disregard for truth. Without openly and honestly submitting our feelings to the Lord, we become vulnerable to an entrenchment in our beliefs based on feelings alone, without regard for their source. Once entrenched, pride may then dig a moat around the deception, causing us to defend it at all cost.

Obsession and Compulsion

The feelings we have may stay with us, affecting our emotions. Because our emotions and our will are closely linked, we may become "driven." An extreme reaction would be an obsession with what God has shown us.

Lacks Specifics

Feelings are often vague. We can feel anxious without knowing why or about what. Feelings of fear don't tell us that we are truly in danger, and if we are, they do not tell us where the threat is coming from. Feelings of compassion for those in need do not tell us how best to help them.

When God gives us feelings we often need more information to know what He is saying. If He causes us to feel peace we might need to know if it is for rest, or if it is to calm us so that we can be more effective or productive.

Affects Us Personally

We can change the way we think more easily than the way we feel. A clerk can probably leave his work at the office, but a hospice worker who cares deeply for her terminally ill patients may find this difficult. When the plight of others touches us, letting go and moving on can be very difficult.

If the Lord speaks to us through "feelings," we may carry it awhile. As an example, when the Lord wants us to pray for an individual, He may use the feelings of concern, compassion or even danger to move us to pray. After praying we may have lingering concern for the person. We may want to do something more. Even when we feel confident God is caring for them, an unsettled feeling may linger.

When we have done all that God is asking of us, He often takes the feeling from us and replaces it with a corresponding feeling: safety replaces danger; peace floods over anxiety. However, if we don't understand how to handle "communication by feelings," we may hold onto the first feeling He gave us. We may reject the following feeling that let's us know we can put it behind us and move on. This is like using the "in" door, but ignoring the "out" door. The feelings remain with us, which is unhealthy.

Instantaneous Or Emerging

Knowing can come suddenly or it can be a growing conviction. When it comes quickly, it often can be strong and intrusive. It may push aside other thoughts and feelings. Thoughts, actions, sights or sounds may prompt it. However, we should not mistakenly assume that these are responsible for the way we feel. We must make allowance for the possibility that it comes from God, even when it coincides with other activities.

The feelings of "knowing" can begin almost imperceptibly and grow over time, sometimes spanning weeks or months until we recognize it as a full-fledged feeling. In contrast to the "sudden knowing" that bursts onto the scene and grabs our attention, we may not acknowledge the "knowing" that develops over time. Much like falling asleep, we are unaware that it is happening until we are jolted awake in realization. Pinpointing when or how it began may be hard. We may only be aware that we have been feeling this way for awhile.

The way that "knowing" occurs (instantaneously or emerging) may vary from person to person and may change from time to time. How it happens is not nearly important as recognizing that it comes from God and is part of the way He speaks to us.

Intuition Or God?

Intuition is defined as "the immediate knowing of something without the conscious use of reasoning."[47] There are many explanations for suddenly "knowing." Mystics refer to it as inner wisdom. Parapsychologists call it extra-sensory perception or ESP. Homespun wisdom reveres "women's intuition." Psychologists and educators talk of the subconscious mind and intuitive reasoning. Norman Simon, the Nobel laureate economist and cognitive scientist, suggested that intuition is nothing more than the brain's capacity for subliminal computation.[48] Another explanation is that it is God communicating with us.

When God causes an unbeliever to "know," they may not understand that He is the source and may look for other explanations. They may even deny God's existence or attribute this knowledge to inner wisdom, ESP, women's intuition or the subconscious mind. When God gives us a "knowing," it does not guarantee that we will acknowledge it is from Him.

Coincidental or Led of the Spirit?

When God gives us feelings, we may act on them without realizing it. We may think it is a remarkable coincidence when we feel like calling a friend, only to find them in dire straits and needing to call someone. As we are led of the Spirit and have remarkable experiences, we may wrongly interpret them as "coincidences." Author/speaker Teresa Seputis brought this issue to my attention in a message she gave in Capetown, South Africa. Her book *How to Hear the Voice of God in a Noisy World* (Charisma House) covers this particular topic in more detail.

When we accept that God speaks through the language of feelings, and when we take time to learn this language, we open a wonderful line of communication with the Lord. Like any language (seeing and hearing included), it has drawbacks. However, by understanding its strengths and weakness, we can use it as God intended and hear God's voice with clarity, consistency and confidence.

16 Thinking the Thoughts of God

I knew something was wrong the moment my wife walked in the door.

I followed Mary back to our bedroom and closed the door. She burst into tears as I sat next to her on the bed, holding and comforting her. She took a deep breath and told me what happened. She was on her way home after picking up our niece from school to spend the afternoon with our children. As she was driving down our narrow, rural road, she approached a jogger on the grassy shoulder. Out from nowhere a dog darted in front of her van. She couldn't swerve for fear of hitting the jogger and had no choice but to hit the dog.

In times of crisis, an amazing amount of detail is etched in our mind. Mary remembered the dog lying motionless at the feet of the jogger, who had a look of disbelief on her face. She remembered feeling the shock of knowing she had just killed an animal. Then came the realization that the dog may belong to the jogger, who had just witnessed the accident. Finally, she saw that our young niece Samantha was chatting away oblivious to what had happened.

Mary's first impulse was to stop, but that would mean eleven-year-old Samantha would see what had happened. Mary feared this would disturb her greatly and continued home with great reluctance. It wasn't until she walked in the house and the sanctuary of our bedroom that she could break down and cry.

I wondered what we should do. Doing nothing seemed heartless. Yet I was concerned that if Mary went back to apologize and explain, an angry owner might lash out at her. The thought came to me to call the sheriff and explain what happened. This thought became a strong desire to call them immediately.

With Mary's consent, I called the sheriff's department and talked to a woman deputy who asked where it had happened. When I told her, she asked if my wife was driving a white van. When I said yes, she said that a deputy was already looking for our vehicle. The dog didn't belong to the jogger, but to a nearby homeowner who saw the whole accident from her front door. She called the sheriff and told the responding officer that her dog had a bad habit of chasing cars. She knew it was just a matter of time before a car hit it. She witnessed the accident and saw that the driver could have done nothing, but called the sheriff because she was hurt and angry that the van didn't stop. She didn't know there was a child inside who might be traumatized.

Once the deputy understood the situation, she assured us there was nothing more we could do. She radioed the information to the responding officer, who returned to the owner and explained why Mary hadn't stopped. The owner also understood and the sheriff called off the search for our white van.

I later went into my home office to send my assistant on an errand in our van. It was then I realized that if I had not made the call, the sheriff's department probably would have stopped my assistant. She would have been driving the white van on the same road. If the sheriff had pulled her over, it would have been upsetting and we all would have had a difficult time getting him to believe what had happened.

God directed my thoughts that day without my realizing it. He dropped the thought in my mind (and the unction in my heart) to call the sheriff . . . immediately.

God Spoke to Luke in the Language of Thought

Something similar apparently happened to Luke, the beloved physician[49] who wrote one of the gospels and the book of Acts. We know, first off, that God directed Luke on what to write because 2 Timothy 3:16 (NKJ) tells us:

All Scripture is given by inspiration of God.

From Luke's perspective, divine inspiration came to him as "it seemed like a good idea." It wasn't an overwhelming spiritual experience, nor was he caught up into the heavenlies. He simply had a thought and it seemed like a good idea to him to write about Jesus Christ.

It seemed fitting for me as well, having investigated everything carefully from the beginning, to write {it} out for you in consecutive order, most excellent Theophilus (Luke 1:3 NAS).

The feel of this verse is that God led Luke to write by planting a seed thought in his mind. It felt as natural to Luke as his own thoughts. So much so that he makes no claim of divine inspiration:

It occurred to me that it would be well to recheck all these accounts from first to last and after thorough investigation to pass this summary on to you (Luke 1:3 TLB).

The phrase "it seemed fitting for me" contains the Greek word dokeo, which means "to be of opinion" (akin to doxa, "opinion") . . . to think, suppose . . to seem, to be reputed"[50]. Jesus used this word when He asked:

What do you think? If a man owns a hundred sheep, and one of them wanders away, will he not leave the ninety-nine on the hills and go to look for the one that wandered off? (Matt. 18:12).

In one commentator's opinion, we can understand Luke as saying "It seemed good, I thought it best; or, I have also determined."[51] In other words, God put thoughts into Luke's mind that he thought were his own.

Perhaps the Lord spoke to David this way:

I will praise the LORD, who counsels me; even at night my heart instructs me (Ps. 16:7).

As with Luke, David's mind and the mind of the Lord "run together."

Having the Mind of Christ

God says He will put His law in our heart and mind:

This is the covenant I will make with them after that time, says the Lord. I will put my laws in their hearts, and I will write them on their minds (Heb 10:16).

He will cause us to understand and be enlightened:[52]

I pray also that the eyes of your heart may be enlightened in order that you may know the hope to which he has called you, the riches of his glorious inheritance in the saints (Eph. 1:18).

In the Old Testament the prophet Isaiah spoke for God when he said:

"For my thoughts are not your thoughts, neither are your ways my ways," declares the LORD. "As the heavens are higher than the earth, so are my ways higher than your ways and my thoughts than your thoughts (Is. 55:8-9).

We could throw our hands in the air in defeat and claim, "There is no way I can ever understand what God wants from me. His thoughts are too lofty, too unattainable!"

I can't understand how God can bother with mere puny man, to pay any attention to him! (Ps. 8:4, TLB).

This could excuse us from the responsibility of discerning the mind of the Lord or even the pressure of trying. But the New Testament presents an entirely different perspective:

For who has known the mind of the Lord that he may instruct him? But we have the mind of Christ (1 Cor. 2:16).

The Living Bible makes this verse come alive!

But, strange as it seems, we Christians actually do have within us a portion of the very thoughts and mind of Christ (1 Cor. 2:16 TLB).

We can now say with confidence that God speaks to us through our thoughts and that He even reveals His thoughts to us!

The supernatural gift of a "word of knowledge" is a manifestation of this:

To one there is given through the Spirit the message of wisdom, to another the message of knowledge by means of the same Spirit (1 Cor. 12:8).

God would speak by putting thoughts, in this case specific knowledge, into the mind of the believer.

God can communicate with us by placing thoughts within us. He did it with Luke to cause him to write the gospel bearing his name. He did it with David. He even does it in personal ways, such as prompting me to call the sheriff. Paul says we have the mind of Christ (1 Cor 3:16). This is a valid, and perhaps common, way for God to speak to us.

Sympathetic Vibration and Fine Tuning

I've never been a musician, but I could see that Gil Melindez certainly was. He opened the lid of the upright piano and, in a strong operatic voice, sang a note into the cabinet. He then thrust the microphone into the piano and lo and behold, the piano strings hummed. Gil was demonstrating sympathetic vibration. He explained that when he sang the note, the strings tuned to that note vibrated without being touched. Because his voice and the strings were tuned together, the vibrations caused by one resonated the other.

We can apply this practice to God placing His thoughts in us, with our minds being like the strings of the piano. When God places His thoughts in us, it is like the singer releasing his voice into the piano. If the strings of our mind are attuned with God, then we will resonate with His voice. The more accurately we are tuned, the better our response. However, if we are out of tune with God and His Word, then His voice might not cause that resonance within us and we won't get God's message.

How can we become fine-tuned to God's voice? Romans 12:2 says:

Do not conform any longer to the pattern of this world, but be trans-formed by the renewing of your mind. Then you will be able to test and approve what God's will is--his good, pleasing and perfect will.

The renewing of the mind transforms us into new instruments. Paul exhorted the Philippians to guard their thoughts:

Finally, brothers, whatever is true, whatever is noble, whatever is right, whatever is pure, whatever is lovely, whatever is admirable-if anything is excellent or praiseworthy-think about such things (Phil. 4:8).

Paul was saying to them to tune the piano strings of their minds. The more closely attuned they were to God's ways, the better they would hear. This admonition is for us today. We must guard our mind so that we can receive the thoughts of God. Our culture exposes us to language that assaults the ears and images that offend the eyes. Without care and diligence, worldly thoughts, ideas and opinions will quickly corrupt our minds.

Speaking into our thoughts can be difficult for God if we have opened our minds to worldly toxins. Yet, the opposite is also true. As we guard our minds and control our thoughts, we present the Lord with a well-tuned piano for Him to play. What accomplished pianist wouldn't prefer to play a finely-tuned instrument? How the Lord must delight in speaking to us when we have the mind of Christ. He renews our minds so we can clearly hear the thoughts He shares with us!

Piggybacking—Thought Upon Thought

We have talked about God putting His thoughts in our mind. However, there is another common way that God uses thoughts. He uses our own thoughts, rather than His, for getting a message through to us. He does this by adding something of His own so that our thoughts take on a new level of meaning. Like a small child riding on the back of an adult, God often piggybacks one of His thoughts onto ours. Together they make His message.

In training seminars I ask people to find a partner. One person in each pair prays for the other, being sensitive to the Lord and paying attention to what he or she is seeing, hearing and feeling. My hope is that as each person prays, God would share something with them about their partner that would bless them or strengthen them in their spiritual walk. After praying, each has time to share what they were hearing, feeling and seeing with their partner.

During a workshop in Rhode Island, one young man confessed to his partner that he wasn't getting anything for her from God. He felt distracted and couldn't concentrate. He explained that he had just come from a great time at the beach and regretted having to leave and come to church. Because the beach was on his mind, it was all he could think of as he prayed for her. He said that when he prayed he saw her on the beach with an onshore wind blowing. It was brisk enough to support her as she leaned into it. These, he apologized, were just his own thoughts because of his preoccupation.

She responded that she needed to hear from God about decisions she was facing. Often when she needed to clear her head and focus on the Lord, she would go to the beach. She knew that in the Bible the wind is sometimes a symbol of the Holy Spirit[53]. She believed that leaning into the wind and being supported by it represented leaning on God in her decisions. He would bear her up and support her. This was very encouraging to her as a reminder that God was there to help! She received a very meaningful message from the Lord by this young man's seemingly undisciplined thoughts.

In this instance, the young man was preoccupied with his own thoughts about the beach. The Lord, as a brilliant Strategist, comfortably inserted a picture of the partner supported by the wind into the young man's thoughts. Without changing the young man's basic train of thought, God added just enough to change the whole meaning and convey a message to the woman. Adding an extra thought to our thoughts is what I mean by "piggybacking."

God may piggyback for several reasons. First, it is efficient. We don't have to clear our mind or take time to quiet our heart. We can offer Him what we have and He can quickly and effectively use it to speak to us. Second, it is easier for us. Some people have strong wills and busy minds. Setting this aside is difficult for them. God works with them by using the thoughts they already have.

Piggybacking is effective, but it is not always ideal. There are times when God wants to say whatever He wants without being forced to piggyback on our thoughts. He wants us to clear our minds and present Him with an open heart. God is a phenomenal Communicator and can speak to us either by giving us His thoughts or by piggybacking on our own.

Putting it Into Practice

Be aware of your thoughts! Take time to notice how your thoughts "wander." Be open to the possibility that God is putting those thoughts there. Luke says that "it occurred to him" to write. What is occurring to you? What might the Lord be saying to you in your thoughts that you think are "just you"?

During your personal prayer time, does your mind sometimes wander? Do you have times when focusing is difficult? When this happens, instead of suppressing your wandering thoughts, see if they have meaning. Maybe the Lord wants to piggyback on your thoughts by adding a thought of His own, talking to you as you talk to Him.

Finally, don't be afraid of your thoughts. We can sometimes get the idea that what we are thinking couldn't possibly be from God. Perhaps we feel this way because often they are not from God. However, we should guard against believing that God cannot speak to us in our minds. Remember, it is God who created our mind. Should we assume it is unsuitable for the Master's use? Quite the contrary. A mind surrendered to the Lord can be an effective instrument for receiving His thoughts.

For who has known the mind of the Lord that he may instruct him? But we have the mind of Christ (1 Cor 2:16).

17 Determining Your Style of Receiving

Celebrating special occasions, taking out the trash and caring for the children all have something in common at my house, romance! ·

Early in our marriage Mary and I tried hard to express our love, but despite our strong commitment to each other we sometimes didn't feel loved. We were good at saying "I love you," but neither of us heard it very well. A friend told us about Gary Chapman's book, *The Five Love Languages*. We learned that if you express love in a way your spouse doesn't understand, they won't realize you've expressed your love at all. The problem is that you're speaking two different love languages[54].

Chapman's book explains the five ways we give and receive affection and calls these "love languages"[55]. I discovered that my primary love language is "words of affirmation." I put my love into words, such as telling my wife how much I love her many times a day.

Mary's love language is "acts of service." She demonstrates love. Both are valid, but we were speaking different languages. I spoke of my love, thinking she heard my message of devotion. She worked hard to communicate her love by many acts of kindness. We were "speaking," but because we were using different languages, we weren't hearing what the other was saying.

Now, to make sure we communicate, we both talk the language of the other. Mary has made heroic efforts to speak her love. She knows the way I receive and she chooses to talk my language. For my part, I take a new view of an overflowing trash can. I no longer see a detestable chore. Now I see a way to show my wife how much she means to me. Don't get me wrong—I'm far from perfect. Mary has done much better than I in changing languages. But I now know that romancing my wife sometimes means celebrating special occasions, taking out the trash and caring for the children!

The Ways We Receive

We differ in the ways we communicate. An auditory person may overlook scowling, restlessness or other visual clues. A visual person may not listen closely to hear what is said. A feeling person may interpret a conversation based on what they "feel" a person is saying, rather than based on their words. When people of different preferences communicate, they may send their messages in ways that their partner can't receive.

Earlier we discussed three primary ways in which God communicates: seeing, hearing and feeling. We can leap forward in our ability to hear God's voice by understanding how we receive best. If we are visual, we may waste time listening for God's voice. We would do much better to look for it.

Which is Best For You?

We use seeing, hearing and feeling to receive from God. We usually prefer one above the others. Discovering our preference is important because this is the most likely way God is speaking to us. Mary chooses to communicate with me in my language rather than her own. She knows how much this means to me. I will get the message more quickly because it is my natural language. I don't have to translate the message from her language to mine before understanding its meaning. God chooses to also speak our language. He knows which language we prefer and He often uses it. The language we prefer is the first place to check when seeking a message from God. However, God loves variety. He created an abundance of languages and He revels in using them all. Learning all the languages for the fullest communication is wise.

Self-Assessment

You may know which language you prefer. Before continuing, record your preference. Keep in mind that you speak all three languages: seeing, hearing and feeling[56]. The one you naturally favor is your primary—or preferred—language. To review "seeing, hearing and feeling" re-read Chapters 7 through 16.

Underline your preferred language:

Seeing   Hearing   Feeling

Please don't continue until you have underlined your preferred language.

Questionnaire

Below is a series of questions designed to help you discover your preferred language. Although you have underlined one above, this may help you discover yourself.

There are three choices for each question. None of the answers are wrong. Please circle all answers that apply to you. You may have more than one answer for a question!

1. When I have leisure time, I prefer to:
    a. watch T.V., a video, or go to the movies.
    b. listen to music, radio, or read books.
    c. do something athletic, physical, or using my hands.

2. What I notice most about people is...
    a. how they look or dress.
    b. how they sound when they talk.
    c. how they move.

3. I learn most easily when, I...
    a. see someone demonstrating what to do.
    b. get verbal instructions.
    c. get "hands-on" experience.

4. When finding my way around a new city I tend to...
    a. use a map.
    b. ask for directions.
    c. trust my feelings about which way to go.

5. I enjoy books or magazines that...
    a. have a lot of pictures.
    b. discuss interesting topics.
    c. cover sports, activities, or crafts.

6. When I have many things to do, I...
    a. make lists for myself or imagine doing them.
    b. keep reminding myself that I have things to do.
    c. feel uncomfortable until all or most of the things are done.

7. When I am talking to someone, I...
   a. try to see what they are saying.
   b. listen closely so that I can hear what they have to say.
   c. try to get in touch with what they are saying.

8. When I solve problems, I...
   a. keep looking at alternatives until the pieces come together.
   b. talk about new approaches until something clicks.
   c. fit possibilities together until I get a feeling of balance.

9. I like any place where:
   a. there are things to see and people to watch.
   b. there is music, conversation, or quiet
   c. there is room to move.[57]

   From "The Motivation Profile," ©2000, by Jay Arthur and Greg Engel

Charting the Results

Add the number of "a" choices. Using the chart titled "Your Results," shade the corresponding number of blocks in the "a" column. Repeat for "b" and "c."

The chart on the left is an example of a person who answered with five a's, two b's and eight c's. Fill the chart on the right with your results.

	Example		
9			
8			■
7			■
6			■
5	■		■
4	■		■
3	■		■
2	■	■	■
1	■	■	■
	a seeing	b hearing	c feeling

	Your Results		
9			
8		✓	
7	✓	✓	
6	✓	✓	
5	✓	✓	
4	✓	✓	✓
3	✓	✓	✓
2	✓	✓	✓
1	✓	✓	✓
	a seeing	b hearing	c feeling

Interpreting the Results

The higher the number in a column, the more you prefer that language. In the example chart, feeling is first with eight boxes shaded. Seeing is second with five. This person is primarily feeling and secondarily seeing. Their preference for hearing is small.

Comparing the Results

Compare your self-assessment with the questionnaire results (chart). If they agree, it suggests that you know your preferred language(s). Focus on them. Talk with the Lord and be attentive to your preferred language(s). He is most likely to respond in the language(s) you prefer. When you discover your preferred language(s) and start using them in talking with God, you may find Him speaking to you extensively. The seeing person may see pictures each time they look. The hearing person may hear His voice in a continual stream of conversation.

I have found that God speaks so much that I can converse with Him continually. At times there is a nonstop flow as we talk. On other occasions He speaks less, but He usually has something to say. Enjoy the incredible flow that discovering your languages(s) releases, and take time to talk with God!

When your self-assessment doesn't agree with the results of the questionnaire, it may mean that you don't understand your preferred language(s). Consider trusting the chart for a time. Experiment with the languages it says are best for you. Take time to speak these languages with God and see if it helps you receive from Him.

If the language you chose in your self-assessment works for you, then don't overestimate the results in the chart. Stick to what works for you. If you are hearing from the Lord, then you have achieved the goal of this book. Whether the language you use agrees with the chart or not is unimportant. However, if you struggle to hear God's voice, then you may have been using the language that isn't best for you. This would be a good time to try out the languages the chart recommends.

Why Were "Thoughts" Not Included?

This book covers four primary languages God uses to communicate with us: thinking, seeing, hearing and feeling (see Chapters 7-16). However, both the self-assessment and the questionnaire omitted the language of thought. For years I have been teaching people how to use the languages of seeing, hearing and feeling to communicate with God. More recently the Lord revealed to me "thinking the thoughts of God." Perhaps with time God will show me how to include thought into the questionnaire.

If you add "thought" to the list how would you rank it among the other three? Is it your preferred language? Is it a secondary language? Perhaps it isn't an important language for you. You may find it helpful to list the four languages in order of importance to you.

God Changes Languages

My personal experience is that God speaks to me in different languages at different times. For a time He communicates almost exclusively in my preferred language of seeing. At other times, He may switch and cause me to hear. It is as if seeing and feeling dry up, and hearing is the only way I can receive. I used to struggle with this, trying to stay in the realm of seeing and feeling. As I learned, I became more comfortable with hearing. I suspect the Lord does this to help me learn the other languages, though I can't be sure. It becomes unimportant as long as I am in communication with Him. You too may find Him switching from language to language. I encourage you to relax and enjoy the experience.

Like a good dance partner, we need to allow God to lead. He may very well take us into areas we would have never considered. Isn't this the whole point? Learning to hear from God so we can know Him more? As we know Him more, our relationship will grow and so will we. Like the proverbial snowball rolling downhill, our experiences increase. We develop positive momentum in our relationship with the Lord. We rapidly begin to hear Him better, know Him more, and become more like Him.

18 The Incredible Benefits of Listening

In his best-seller Hunt for Red October author Tom Clancy describes how submarines communicate with their land bases. To avoid detection, submarines remain submerged much of the time. This strategy has the disadvantage of preventing them from receiving satellite signals that cannot penetrate sea water effectively. To overcome this, the U.S. Navy uses an Extremely Low Frequency radio signal, or ELF.

The ELF reaches deep into the oceans around the world and because of this is well-suited for sending signals to submarines out at sea. It is limited because it can transmit only one character approximately every thirty seconds. This slow rate of transmission makes it impractical for sending anything but the shortest messages. It is typically used as a "bell ringer" to alert the submarine to surface just long enough to communicate via satellite, then return to relative safety in the depths of the sea.

In Clancy's book the surfaced submarine sends its messages to the satellite using a laser. This "digital burst" of information takes a fraction of a second; dramatically reducing the time the submarine must remain on the surface and be vulnerable to detection.

God's "ELF" Signal Can Reach Us

Have you ever tried talking with the Lord, but did not get a response? How often have you asked a question, but did not receive an answer? Have you ever had a difficult situation in life when you cried out to hear from God, only to hear silence? Have you fasted, prayed and petitioned heaven for an answer, but heard nothing? In great need the awakened soul asks, "Why God?"

Like that submerged submarine out of reach of the satellite signal, we may submerge ourselves deeply in our own life and self interests. We often become busy and distant, doing our own thing in our own way. We bury ourselves, submerged below the level of communication, unable to hear from God.

God's solution is comparable to the Navy's ELF signal that reaches great depths in any ocean, though it communicates very slowly. God, in His steadfast love, sends us messages that can reach us no matter how deeply absorbed and off-course we are. These, too, can be very slow and may take us a lifetime to receive.

God's ELF signals are trials, tribulations, and life experiences. By taking us through difficult experiences, the Lord gets our attention. He may dry up our finances, remove grace for getting along with others, take us into a spiritual wilderness, or any number of things that cause us to feel discomfort. Like the ELF, this type of "signal" from God gets our attention. It reaches us no matter where we are in life, but it can be very slow in communicating a message.

When we are going through tough times, we press into God, asking Him, "What is happening? I need you Lord!" We have just tuned into His ELF signal. We acknowledge that God is sending us a message, but we do not understand what the message is. We ask God to tell us what to do, but no amount of pleading speeds up the message. God's ELF signal of using difficult experiences is incapable of sending a fast message. If this is the only signal we listen to, it will take us a very long time to discern God's will.

So why doesn't He just tell us?

God's Digital Burst

Communicating by satellite is much more efficient for the submarine. It can send and receive lengthy messages very quickly using "digital bursts."

God has "digital burst" communication with His children. It is His voice within us. He can clearly and quickly tell us everything we need to know to fulfill His will and purposes. What would our lives be like if we regularly had "digital burst" communication with Him? What would it be like if we could talk with the Lord conversationally just as we talk with each other? What impact would clear communication have on our prayer life?

Why doesn't God stop sending us ELF through life experiences and use His voice within us?

Coming Up Higher and Being Vulnerable

To send and receive digital burst communication, the submarine must surface and be vulnerable to detection. It is in this situation that it can lock onto the satellite signal and benefit from clear, fast communication.

In order for God to speak quickly and clearly within us, we too must "surface" and be vulnerable. We must decide that we want to "come up higher" in God. We must leave the depths of our self interests and rise to the heights of a life controlled and directed by God. We must then choose to become "vulnerable" to Him.

When we open up ourselves to hearing directly, we are apt to hear all kinds of things. God may want to speak to us about our lifestyle, our eating habits, our spiritual disciplines or other issues we may not want to talk about.

We have to be vulnerable to Him. We must be willing to hear whatever God has to say and trust He has our very best interests at heart. If we do not really want to hear what the Lord has to say then we return to the depths of our self-life, insulating and protecting ourselves from His voice.

Can't He Tell Us If He Really Wants To?

When God is sending us an ELF message through difficult circumstances we do not understand, we try to bargain with Him. We promise to pray more, read our Bibles or be better Christians, if He will, just this once, answer us clearly and directly. The issue is not that God is unwilling, but like the submerged submarine, we have not positioned ourselves correctly for direct communication.

He may be sending the message both ways, by ELF (our circumstances) and by digital burst (His voice within). But if we have not positioned ourselves properly by "surfacing," we cannot get the digital burst He is sending.

In this way we choose the manner of communication, the slow ELF signal of trials, tribulations and life experiences, or the digital burst of His direct voice. ELF is not His preferred method, but in His mercy He uses it. When this happens we again ask God to "just tell us" what He is trying to say.

Learning to Receive Digital Burst Communication

Each of us can receive God's digital bursts because of how He created us.[58] If we correctly position ourselves, like the surfaced submarine, we can receive His digital bursts.

We can do two important things to position ourselves properly: 1.)
We can stir up the desire to hear; and 2.) We can deal with the fear
of hearing.

Stirring Up the Desire to Hear

"Where there's a will there's a way" is true regarding hearing
God's voice. We must cultivate a will to hear and stir up a desire and
passion to communicate with the Lord. These desires and feelings are
often a result of our thoughts.

Try this exercise: take a moment and think about a dear, close
friend. What is it about them that you appreciate? What is it that
endears you to them? After just a few minutes, you will probably
begin to experience warm feelings of love, appreciation, or respect.
Our heart responds to our thoughts. We can also stir up our desire to
hear God's voice by thinking about why hearing is important, or
remembering who He is.

**Ponder the following thoughts to stir up your desire to hear God's
voice:**

- What would your life be like if you could hear from God clearly,
  consistently and confidently?
- What would it be like if, when facing a problem, you could
  immediately hear what God had to say about it?
- How would hearing God's voice affect your relationships, your
  parenting, your marriage and your business dealings?
- How exciting would it be to discover your purpose in life and
  begin to fulfill your destiny?
- Would you like to experience healing of past hurts and disap-
  pointments as you listen to His loving voice minister to you?
- Would you like to know what is holding you back from fully
  serving God and learn how to overcome so you can walk in victory?
- Do you want to hear God's words of mercy, love and grace
  drawing you to Him?
- Do you want the Lord to reveal Himself to you so that you can
  receive everything you need to fulfill your destiny?[59]

- Are you interested in communicating with your heavenly Father, Friend and Bridegroom, to build an intimate relationship?
- Think about your desire to see the Lord enthroned in heaven, to walk and talk with Him and to be the apple of His eye. You can begin right here, right now. Take a few minutes and talk to Him.

Stir up your desires and keep on stirring them. Move with action and purpose to hear His voice in every area of your life.

Dealing With the Fear of Hearing

Our carnal heart is evil and imagines all kinds of wickedness. Jeremiah put it this way:

The heart is deceitful above all things and beyond cure. Who can understand it? (Jer. 17:9).

Solomon, in his great wisdom, also recognized this:

This is the evil in everything that happens under the sun: The same destiny overtakes all. The hearts of men, moreover, are full of evil and there is madness in their hearts while they live, and afterward they join the dead (Eccl. 9:3).

Jesus, the ultimate Giver of truth, validates Jeremiah and Solomon:

For out of the heart come evil thoughts, murder, adultery, sexual immorality, theft, false testimony, slander (Matt. 15:19).

This does not mean that everything about people is evil, or that we personally are evil. God created each of us with wonderful qualities and intends for us to "live out of" this part of our nature. Without God this is not possible because Adam's sin in the Garden of Eden affected the human race and all mankind. From him we inherited a carnal, sinful nature that is constantly at war with God. We can choose to allow God to rule us or we can allow our sinful nature to rule us.[60]

It is God's desire that we yield ourselves to Him and serve Him. When we do, His power gives us the ability to overcome our sinful nature and become the wonderful person He created us to be.

Who has not gone through a painful or tragic experience, only to blame God for not helping or protecting them? Our sinful nature often accuses God. How often have we been afraid of what God will ask of us if we completely surrender to Him? Will He call us to be missionaries, living in a mud hut and eating grubs? Will He ask us to give all our money to the poor? Will He remove the comforts of life and ask us to live a monastic life? Will He ask us to be fools for Christ by preaching the gospel on the street?

There is no end to the fears our heart presents us about God. If we believe these fears, we will be reluctant to listen to God. We become afraid to hear and we resist surrendering to Him.

We may also ignore God to avoid saying "no" to Him. As Adam and Eve hid in the Garden, we exercise deafness so that we will not hear what we do not want to hear. Is it any wonder that many people struggle to hear God's voice? When we are afraid of what He will say, we will continue to struggle to hear His voice.

I didn't know that I was afraid of what God would say to me. Occasionally, when I asked the Lord what I should preach, He wouldn't answer. I was left to decide on my own. I felt very uncomfortable making the decision myself, as if I were doing what seemed right to me, rather than what seemed right to God. A Proverb came to mind:

> There is a way that seems right to a man, but in the end it leads to death (Prov. 14:12).

I would have been much more comfortable had God told me the subject He wanted me to speak on. Years later I understood that at those times He did not want me to prepare. He wanted me to speak spontaneously and allow Him to give me the words as I was preaching. At the time I was afraid to admit it, even to myself, so I ignored Him as He instructed me about what I should do. The only thing I was willing to discuss with Him was the subject of the sermon. Since God was not talking about this, I felt as if He were not speaking to me.

The solution to this dilemma is to see God as He really is, rather than how our heart wrongly perceives Him. He is good and everything He does is good.

> You are good, and what you do is good; teach me your decrees (Ps. 119:68).

He is not trying to hurt us.

> For he does not willingly bring affliction or grief to the children of men (Lam. 3:33).

His love for us is so strong that He is in heaven, dancing over us in excitement about blessing us and bringing us into our promised land! Did you know this is in the Bible?

*The LORD your God is with you, he is mighty to save. He will take
great delight in you, he will quiet you with his love, he will rejoice over
you with singing (Zeph. 3:17).*

"Rejoice" is the Hebrew word giyl and means "properly, to spin
round (under the influence of any violent emotion, i.e. usually
rejoice, or (as cringing) fear."[61] As God rejoices over us, He spins
about (dances over us) under the violent emotions of love and passion.

*I will rejoice in doing them good and will assuredly plant them in this
land with all my heart and soul (Jer. 32:41).*

When feeling safe and secure in God's tender loving care, we will
not fear what He will do to us. This allows us to drop our resistance
and causes us to come running into the arms of the One who loves
us so much.

This is like the submarine coming to the surface and being vulnerable. We come up out of the depths or our self-life and we come up
higher in God. We become vulnerable and we position ourselves to
hear clearly, consistently and confidently.

19 Sharpening Your Hearing Through Relationship

Mary and I met in Bible college and soon became good friends. Late one autumn evening we found ourselves strolling through a quaint rural area on the outskirts of San Antonio. A stirring breeze shuffled the fall leaves through the street as one street light punctuated the night. The arching trees provided a romantic canopy.

Everything to the contrary, we were not romantically involved. We were best friends and in times like this enjoyed sharing our hopes, dreams and visions of the future. We talked about our families, our aspirations in the ministry, and about the Lord. On this particular quiet fall evening the tranquility was shattered when a dog suddenly bolted toward us. He had apparently been lying still in the middle of the street, obscured by the darkness. He waited until we were within feet before springing to attack.

Courage, as you already know, is not my strongest quality. Nevertheless I rose to the challenge and instantly jumped in front of Mary to protect her. My knees were bent slightly, my feet apart and my hands outstretched. I braced for the lunge of "mad dog." I amazed even myself with my heroic and selfless act of courage. As I considered my next course of action, Mary began to laugh. Her response confused me, and then I saw why: "mad dog" wasn't a dog at all, but a large piece of cardboard blown up off the street by the wind. I was fending off the attack of a flattened box.

I casually stood up, put my hands in my pockets and resumed my stroll as if I had known all along it was only cardboard. I'm glad it was dark so Mary couldn't see my embarrassed face.

The incident, however, caused me to reflect on how I really felt about Mary. She was the one I wanted to spend time with and share my innermost feelings with. Before we had any romantic feelings for each other, we were close and dear friends. Before I kissed her for the first time or even held her hand, we had spent several years together building our friendship.

Mary and I fondly recall our college days and all our long soulful chats. In our marriage we have learned that talking honestly and lovingly is one of the most important pillars of a relationship.

Communications Builds Relationship

I sometimes watch other couples in restaurants and notice how they relate to each other. Some will sit in silence, sharing only an occasional word. Other times the husband is absorbed in a newspaper while his wife stares off into the distance. Though married, they show little sign of being connected. Other couples are a study in the strength of marriage. Not only do they talk, but they seem genuinely interested in each other. They make eye contact, respond to each other and obviously enjoy each other's company and linger there with each other for as long as possible.

The Lord wants us to linger with Him. He surprised me during one of my prayer times. I had only a few minutes, but I wanted to spend them with Him. I asked Him to reveal Himself to me based on Philippians 3:10, which is one of my life verses:

That I may know Him and the power of His resurrection, and the fellowship of His sufferings, being conformed to His death. (NKJV)

As I prayed what I believed to be an honorable prayer for a revelation of God, I heard the Lord say to me, "I'm not a harlot." I was taken aback. His tone and abruptness were shocking—it was like a slap in the face. I listened and He continued, "You rush in and out of prayer like a revolving door and spend very little time with Me. You ask Me to reveal Myself to you, but I'm not a harlot and I don't get a thrill from exposing Myself. I am chaste. If you want me to reveal Myself, you have to spend quality time with Me."

It was true. I had developed a habit of rushing in and out of prayer. I was fulfilling an obligation, but I wasn't giving of myself. I would go through the fast food drive-thru of my prayer closet and order one powerful revelation of God with a side of fries and a drink. The Lord set me straight that He was honorable, and that intimacy and a revelation of Him were based on relationship.

God is an awesome Lover who takes our breath away in a time of intimacy. Yet only at the right time and place because He is pure and virtuous. He unveils Himself in a way that makes our head swim with delight, but only in the secret place with His true love. He made His point, and I repented.

Friendship: A New and Deeper Communication

Jesus gave His disciples an interesting perspective on relationship and communication. It's found in John 15:15:

> I no longer call you servants, because a servant does not know his master's business. Instead, I have called you friends, for everything that I learned from my Father I have made known to you.

This verse reveals three dynamics of Jesus' relationship with the disciples:

First, Jesus had a master/servant relationship with His disciples.

Second, the relationship underwent change; it became a friendship. It changed from an authoritative relationship to a personal and intimate one.

Third, it identifies the catalyst for change: communication.

Jesus revealed to His disciples the intimate secrets His Father had been telling Him. The nature of His communication changed the nature of His relationship–from master/servant to friendship.

Would you like a deeper relationship with God? Is it your desire to be one of those that dwells in the secret place of the Most High and abides under the shadow of the Almighty? Then understand and receive what Jesus taught His disciples in John 15:15, what the Lord taught me in my drive-thru prayer time, and what Mary and I learned on those long walks in college: Communication builds relationships.

Relationship Increases Communication

The reciprocal of this axiom is also true. Relationship increases communication.

Our relationship with Him must be deepened for the Lord to communicate more. Spending quality time with Him, surrendering to His will, and talking with Him increases our relationship.

God Promises to Reveal Himself to Us

In God's Word we see a direct connection between communication and relationship. John 10:27 begins with communication. Jesus said "My sheep hear my voice." Then He mentions relationship when He says, "and I know them, and they follow me."

The reason we hear God's voice is that we know Him. We believe in Him as Lord and trust Him. This covenant relationship opens the lines of communication, and He speaks to us. What would it be like to hear God pour out His heart? What if He shared those things that are near and dear to Him? Moses heard Him[62]. So did Abraham and Enoch. God is capable of deep communication if we are willing to enter a deep relationship.

John 15:15 contains a direct connection between communication and relationship. The disciples' relationship with Jesus changed from a servant/master relationship to a friendship because of communication. Hebrews 10:22 says,

> Let us draw near to God with a sincere heart in full assurance of faith, having our hearts sprinkled to cleanse us from a guilty conscience and having our bodies washed with pure water.

Demonic Communication

In seminars I instruct audiences in spiritual exercises designed to give them an opportunity to listen to the Lord. Invariably, someone will express the concern that the voice they are listening for may not be from God. They want assurance that they are not opening up themselves to demons.

I assure them that we have a clearly defined relationship with the Lord, and we can expect Him to speak to us (John 10:27). It is safe to let down our guard and receive from the Lord because of the communication/relationship principle. We have a very limited relationship with the devil, so we have limited communication with him.

Answering the following questions can help bring more clarity: Who are you in covenant with—God or the devil? Whose child are you—God's or the devil's? Who are you in relationship with—God or the devil? Finally, whose voice will you hear—God's or the devil's? Answer: God's!

It is because we are in relationship with God that we will hear His voice. Because we don't have relationship with the devil, we don't expect to hear His voice. We do have a form of interaction with the devil and his demons—as victors to the vanquished, conquerors to the conquered and overcomers to the overcome.

Our communication is "get thee behind me Satan!" and he has to obey. This is the communication/relationship principle in action. Though demons may tempt us, we who love God can easily deal with it. James 4:7 says, "Submit yourselves, then, to God. Resist the devil, and he will flee from you." We can't stop demons from trying to tempt us, but we can stop them from gaining a foothold in our lives.

Some Christians May Still be at Risk

We have every reason to feel safe and secure as we communicate with the Father. However, be aware of some exceptions that can make us vulnerable to demonic deception. If we have one of these areas in our lives that we have not dealt with, the enemy has an open door. He may come to us as an angel of light, deceiving us into believing that we are hearing from God. It is vital that we recognize and deal scripturally with these areas. At the end of this section, ministry steps have been provided for cleansing, forgiveness, and closing the door to any spirit other than the Lord Jesus. When this is done, these doors are closed to the enemy.

Open Doors for Demonic Communication

Involvement in the Occult

Some Christians, before surrendering their lives to the Lord, were involved in occult activity. Jesus saves and delivers us from this just as completely as He does from everything else. However, when a person has attempted to contact the spirit realm through any means other than through the Lord, they open the door for demonic communication. This includes seances, Ouija boards, conjuring up spirits, contacting spirit guides and other forms of contacting the spirit realm. Even seemingly harmless childhood games that pretend to conjure the dead can open the door to demons, as can having your palm read or your fortune told. Even if this was done simply as entertainment at a fair or carnival, it can open a door to demons.

Continual, Willful Rebellion

Another sin that could give demons a foothold is continual, willful rebellion. This is not the occasional attitude of resistance or a difficult adolescence (although these can lead to the sin of rebellion if they are not dealt with). Continual, willful rebellion resists authority in any form. This person often has difficulty with teachers, parents, employers, law enforcement, government or any form of authority. A person in rebellion often realizes they have a problem, but they continue in it nonetheless.

If this sin is continual and willful and casts off rightful authority given for protection, it leaves us vulnerable and unprotected. The

Bible likens it to witchcraft, "For rebellion [is as] the sin of witchcraft, and stubbornness [is as] iniquity and idolatry" (1 Sam. 15:23).

Only God knows the heart of man. If you feel as if this might apply to you, I strongly recommend the ministry steps at the end of this chapter. Pray through them to completely deal with this sin. Before you do, you must be prepared to forsake rebellion in all its forms. You must accept the authority of God in your life and all lawful authority He places over you.

Habitual, Unrepented Sin

The Bible is clear that we have sinned:

For all have sinned and fall short of the glory of God (Rom. 3:23).

Yet it is not sin that prevents us from talking to God or that opens the door to demonic communication. After all, Adam had a lengthy conversation with God from behind the bush after eating the forbidden fruit. His sin didn't keep him from talking to God. Neither did Eve's innocence protect her from hearing Satan as the serpent beguiled her. Sin alone is not the issue.

When we knowingly continue in a sin, refusing to turn away from it, and justify it, we open the door to demons. Any sin we refuse to repent of and willfully entertain opens the door to the enemy. Demons are attracted to sin like flies to a dumpster. It is essential we keep ourselves clean by the blood of Jesus.

Closing the Door to Demonic Communication

Jesus restores and sets us free from demonic activity. He cleansed us from sin through His shed blood on Calvary. If you have opened the door to demon communication through occult activity, rebellion, or habitual, unrepented sin, you can take action now to close that door. Pray through the following ministry steps of confessing, forgiving, repenting and renouncing.

If you are not a Christian, surrendering your life to the Lord is first. Please see Appendix to learn what it means to be a Christian. The appendix will also lead you in salvation by surrendering your life to God. Then, return to the following ministry steps.

Ministry Steps[63]

To prevent demonic communication, closing the doors discussed in this chapter is important. The following ministry steps are explained and there is a sample prayer for you to personalize. When done from the heart, these will close the door to demonic communication. They are also helpful in other areas of sin. Allow the Holy Spirit to show you any areas of your life with which He would like to deal.

Confess:

Admit your sin to the Lord. Don't justify it or make it sound less sinful than it is. Honestly and openly admit to it and take responsibility for it. 1 John 1:9 says:

If we confess our sins, he is faithful and just and will forgive us our sins and purify us from all unrighteousness.

Forgive:

There are three aspects of forgiveness:

1.) Ask God to forgive you of your sin. Jesus shed His sinless blood on the cross to forgive your sins. There is no sin more powerful than the blood of Jesus. No matter what you have done, the blood of Jesus is more powerful. He is willing and able to forgive you.

2.) You must forgive others for any way they contributed to your sin. Perhaps your sin of rebellion is due in part to an evil father. You need to forgive him. When we forgive others, it doesn't mean that what they did is OK. It doesn't mean they are free to do it to us again. What it does mean is that you give them a pardon. That is what for-give-ness means, giving beforehand. We are giving a pardon to them before God judges them just as Jesus pardons us. If we fail to forgive others, the Lord won't forgive us.

For if you forgive men when they sin against you, your heavenly Father will also forgive you. But if you do not forgive men their sins, your Father will not forgive your sins (Matt. 6:14-15).

If you have been deeply offended, this may be difficult, but it is necessary. Ask the Lord for strength, grace, mercy and anything else you need. He will empower you to forgive.

3.) You also must forgive yourself. The Lord is not pleased when we continue to see ourselves as guilty once He has forgiven us, or when we beat ourselves up over our past. When Jesus saves us and forgives us, He gives us His own righteousness (Rom. 4: 5-6, 24-25).

The words *"it was credited to him"* were written not for him alone *[Abraham], but also for us, to whom God will credit righteousness-for*

*us who believe in him who raised Jesus our Lord from the dead. He was
delivered over to death for our sins and was raised to life for our justi-
fication (Rom. 4:22-25).*

No matter what we have done, once God forgives us, we have the
righteousness of Jesus Christ. In God's eyes we are as righteous as
Jesus is because we have Jesus' righteousness. We must renew our
minds to see ourselves just as God sees us: righteous.

Repent:

To repent means "to turn away from." After receiving forgiveness
for our sins, we must turn away from them so we don't enter into
them again. This doesn't mean we will never sin, but it does mean we
have made a choice to forsake sin and follow God. We must forsake
occult activity, rebellion, and habitual, willful sin.

Renounce:

Renouncing means to break a legal agreement. Chester and Betsy
Kylstra, in their excellent book Restoring the Foundations, liken it to
breaking a contract. When we sin, we have come into agreement
with sin and the devil. Now we must break that agreement. We do
this by renouncing it.

A Sample Prayer:

All of the above steps are included in the following prayer. I
encourage you to pray this prayer from your heart using your own
words. Fill in the blanks to personalize it for yourself and name each
sin or person where shown before continuing on.

> *"Father, I confess the sin of involvement in the occult, rebellion,
> and unrepented sin (say those that apply). I admit to these sins
> and I ask You to forgive me. Apply the blood of Jesus to me and
> wash away every sin of which I am guilty. I forgive (name the per-
> son) for (say they how offended you). [Repeat this for each person
> before continuing on]. I forgive myself and I will no longer hold
> this against myself.*
>
> *"Lord, I repent. I turn away from these sins and I forsake them. I
> choose instead to follow You. I renounce these sins of (name them)
> and I break all legal agreement I had with them. In Jesus' Name.
> Amen!"*

Pray

Close the doors to any demonic communication by praying the above prayer. Or, use your own words to confess, forgive, repent and renounce. You may wish to have someone with you for support, encouragement and comfort. You may find it helpful to write your prayer and then have someone to lead you through it as you speak with the Lord. Please keep in mind that God looks at our heart. Repeating the words of a prayer that we don't mean won't help us. Sincerity is essential. Pray from your heart.

For More Information

If you would like more information about deliverance and freedom from the occult, I recommend the following:

Restoring the Foundations (Book)
Proclaiming His Word Ministry
P.O. Box 2339
Santa Rosa Beach, FL 32459
850-835-4060
www.phw.org (online store)

Evangel Christian Churches (deliverance seminar)
28491 Utica Road
Roseville, MI 48066
810-773-6568

20 When Wills Collide

It doesn't get much better than this. I was walking along our beautiful, white sandy beach of Florida's Gulf Coast, enjoying an early morning quiet time with the Lord. I had the beach all to myself, praying and taking in the grandeur of my surroundings.

These wonders of creation so moved me that I found myself worshipping and surrendering to God in a whole new way. His presence felt so real, so strong. It was exciting to be in this "secret place" with Him. I could barely contain my joy and awe at walking and talking with the Lord.

I wanted to go deeper in this wonderful experience. As I watched the small waves gently caress the beach, I kicked off my shoes and plunged into the surf. The warm water felt wonderful in contrast to the cool air as I bobbed among the gentle ocean swells. I felt as if I was joining with nature to praise Him for His wonderful works and awesome ways. I exulted in Him. I couldn't restrain my shouts of joy as the seawater both soothed and massaged my body. I felt at one with God and His creation.

Thankfully, no one else was around! It must have made quite a sight. I totally abandoned dignity as I gave my all to Him.

After quite some time I felt emotionally and physically spent and returned to the beach to recover, staying in the presence of the Lord. As my hands dug idly in the sand, I poured out my heart to God. For the past few weeks I had been meeting with Him on this beach. I was making an extra spiritual push in a desire to launch into a higher realm of my destiny. I desperately wanted to come up higher in my relationship with God and in His call on my life.

As I poured out my heart to God, I moved beyond carefully crafted prayers and cried out from my heart. I stopped thinking about
what I was saying and found myself expressing the raw feelings of my
heart. Without being aware of it, I began to complain about the slow
spiritual progress I was making. I felt I had ministered in relative
obscurity for years and was discouraged that this book wasn't finished. I was disappointed that radio and T.V. appearances were rare.
I complained that I hadn't preached to the multitudes in stadiums
and mega-churches.

God then interrupted me and said, "You love the praises of man."
This one short comment cut me to the core. He laid bare my hidden
motive to be seen and admired. For years I wanted to be in the public eye. My need for affirmation joined forces with my desire to be in
the limelight. The result was that I wanted to preach to the thousands
and be applauded. I wanted to make it to the "big time" so that my
name would be a household word and I could point to my success
and feel good about who I was.

It was this mess of corrupt motives that God exposed when He
said, "You love the praises of man." In that moment I faced the truth
that much of my ministry efforts were directed toward achieving
fame and success. I could no longer hide from myself the fact that
many of my deep, primary motivations as a minister came from selfish desires that displeased the Lord. On an isolated beach that early
morning, I wept and repented.

How did I get here? How had I come all this way in years of ministry and not dealt with this? How could I have harbored these sinful
motives for so long and be unaware of them? The truth is, I had
known for a long time. I knew I was caught up in performance and
achievement and wanted to feel valuable and important as a person.
I knew this was wrong, but rather than confront it and change, I hid
from it. I pretended it wasn't there.

Countless times God had spoken to me about it, but I just turned
away, pretending not to hear. Occasionally, during a relaxing
moment, these motives would poke their head up into my awareness.
I knew if I acknowledged their existence, I would have to deal with
them and I didn't want to do that.

Somewhere in the depths of my heart I thought fame would give
me the approval and affirmation I so desperately wanted. In the hope
of feeling good about myself, I longed for the approval of others.

Because my need felt so great, I wanted constant reassurance from as many people as possible. I thought I would gain that approval if I had exposure through books, T.V., radio and large churches.

If God denied me this type of ministry, I felt I would be doomed to a life of painfully low self-esteem. This prospect was so horrible that I refused to consider it. I set my course for fame and popularity. But my will was on a collision course with the will of God.

For years I ministered without coming to grips with my inner drive to succeed and be famous. Thankfully, God gave me the grace to be obedient to Him one day at a time. My actions were in the will of God even if some of my motives were not.

It was only after I made a fresh dedication to the will of God that I received healing. It all started that day on the beach as I walked and prayed to seek a deeper relationship with Him and a greater fulfillment of my destiny. After His startling words, "You love the praises of man," there was no more hiding or avoiding the issue. God exposed it in all its ugliness. Like a child caught with his hand in the cookie jar, there was no denying my sin. Through a torrent of tears I confessed and repented.

God graciously ministered to me that only His love gives me value, not love from others. I received the truth that we are who we are by the grace of God. We are fearfully and wonderfully made. A wonderful thing happened: I started to believe in Christ in me.

His mercy, grace and healing changed my heart and no longer am I driven to succeed. Now my passion is doing the will of God. Whatever He chooses for me to do, I want to bring joy to His heart through obedience. There is a fulfillment and reward that comes from surrendering to Him that nothing else can give. I believe this is one of the first steps to "joy unspeakable and full of glory," or as 1 Peter 1:8 (TLB) says:

You love him even though you have never seen him; though not seeing him, you trust him; and even now you are happy with the inexpressible joy that comes from heaven itself.

This joy is so incredible that it can't be described. It left me yearning for a way to express it that morning on the beach. Plunging into the wonderfully warm and clear water was an act of celebrating God and His work in my life.

How does this apply to hearing God's voice? During the many years I ignored my wrong motives for fame and popularity, the Lord was gently speaking to me. That morning on the beach was not the first time He had tried to heal me. He had been whispering to me in a thunderous way for a long time. Yet because I had set my will to attain fame and success, I didn't want to surrender to His will. I wrongly felt that I couldn't emotionally afford to give this up.

At the same time, I didn't want to blatantly rebel against God. Like Adam, I chose to hide. Not only did I hide from the problem, I hid from God. I refused to acknowledge His dealings in this area of my life. As peculiar as it seems, I surrendered other areas of my life to the Lord and could clearly hear Him speak in these areas. It was in this one area that I pretended I was deaf. It is hard to say how much time I wasted hiding from God. I do know that as long as my will was against His, it drastically impaired my ability to hear Him. Once I yielded to Him and received His forgiveness and healing, my hearing ears became remarkably sensitive.

If your will is on a collision course with God's, don't avoid Him. Open your heart to Him and allow Him to change your will. In the Lord's Prayer, Jesus prayed "Thy kingdom come, thy will be done." Allow God's will to be done in your life.

If you need to surrender your will to God like I did on the beach that morning, simply pray a prayer like the following one:

"Father, I confess that my will has been in conflict with Your will. Please forgive me and wash me clean with the blood of Jesus. I surrender my will to You and I accept Your will in every area of my life. Lord, please speak to me. I would like to hear what You have to say to me, particularly in those areas where my will was against Yours. I open up my heart to hear whatever You have to say. Amen"

Take a few moments and listen. I have found that nothing cleans out the ears like surrender!

21 Practicing Deafness

Have you ever ignored God? Ever pretended you didn't hear Him?

I have driven over the speed limit. I have overindulged at the dinner table and spoken harshly to my wife. I have done many things I shouldn't have. Frequently the Lord has spoken to me to slow down, eat less, and treat my wife like a queen. Sometimes I have responded in obedience, sometimes I have not.

When I disobey, I hear God gently coaching me, calling me back to obedience. When I set my heart to do what I want, I find it's less painful if I shut out the voice of the Lord. The love and kindness in His voice is too hard to hear when I choose not to obey. In these times I work hard at ignoring His voice and shutting Him out.

Perhaps, in the words of the Apostle Paul, I am the worst of sinners (1 Tim 1:18). Perhaps I am the only one who has ever deliberately ignored God and wanted Him to stop convicting me of my disobedience. However, I suspect that one or two others might also have done this. It is for these that this chapter is intended.

How ironic that we want to hear God's voice, yet sometimes we try so hard to ignore it. We busy ourselves in hopes of being distracted from what He is saying. We immerse ourselves in a diversion and cannot spare one bit of our attention for the Lord. Perhaps someone offended us. When we think about them, we hear the Lord whispering we need to forgive them. Instead, we quickly move onto other things and force this into the basement of our heart where we forbid God's revealing light to shine.

It would be interesting to know how the average Christian responds to God's voice while the offering is being taken at church! How often have we been unwilling to give what God is telling us to? Rather than simply obeying, we busy ourselves looking for the checkbook or finding money for the children to give.

Is it any wonder we have difficulty hearing God's voice when we spend so much time trying to ignore it? I practiced spiritual deafness and became pretty good at it. Of course, I never would have admitted it at the time. The simple truth was I often didn't want to hear from God so I learned to tune Him out. I became an expert at spiritual deafness! If a serious need arose in my life and I couldn't handle it, I inevitably blamed God for not telling me what to do or for not showing me the way out. I practiced deafness, but blamed God when I couldn't hear.

This creates a dilemma for us when we aren't ready to obey God in every area of our life. Eventually in our relationship with the Lord, an area of our life will come up in which we are not prepared to surrender to Him. We may be tempted to return to old habits and start practicing deafness again.

There is a better way! Rather than turning a deaf ear, listen. Hear what God has to say. It may be incredibly painful. It may hurt when we have to be honest with ourselves and with God and say "I don't want to give this up." Rather than trying to spare ourselves pain by plugging our ears, listen.

Ultimately each of us must choose when we will surrender and obey. We know the sooner we do it the better. However, even when we are struggling to surrender, we can still listen. All it will cost us is our comfort. What we will gain is a sensitive ear and a responsive heart. I am not recommending you disobey God. What I am suggesting is that if you are going to disobey anyway, listening is better than practicing deafness.

It is better to have a hearing ear and sensitive heart—even if it costs us our comfort. Hardening our heart is far worse and deafens our ear, only to gain a measure of artificial peace.

I want to encourage those who might be struggling with opening their heart to the Lord. Listen to what He has to say. When God speaks, it is not to bring you misery, but to lead you into His life. He wants to heal you, free you, and give you joy that is so good you can't describe it:

> *Though you have not seen him, you love him; and even though you do not see him now, you believe in him and are filled with an inexpressible and glorious joy (1 Pet. 1:8).*

When we open our heart and ears to the Lord, He may surprise us with the wonderful things He says. I have found that His voice is loving far more often than it is harsh. Why wait until something serious happens and then blame God because you were unable to hear from Him? Why not let this very issue be the "something serious?" Why not listen now and learn to hear?

I pray God speaks to you in areas where you have been avoiding Him. I pray He manifests Himself to you as a loving God with freedom, deliverance and healing. I pray you not only learn to hear His voice, but that His voice sets you free! Listen and begin walking in victory, freedom and life!

22 Breaking Off Communication

I was busy packing for an out-of-town trip to Canada the following morning. All I needed was to simply make a copy of a cassette tape. I had a blank tape handy and programmed the computer for printing the label.

I went into the living room to put the tape into the stereo. What, no stereo? Oh, right. We had replaced it, but the new one didn't have a cassette deck. I brought the old one in from the garage only to find that the speaker wire was cut. The simplest task was now becoming frustrating and time-consuming. I spliced some wires and everything worked correctly.

Now for the label. As I typed the title into the computer, everything on the screen scattered. It took the better part of an hour to fix. By this time I was unbelievably behind. We had dinner guests coming over that evening and I needed to get to bed early because I had a 5 a.m. flight. It was only by the grace of God that I wasn't completely stressed out. Now all I had to do was print.

Then I remembered: I couldn't print—the computer network was down and with it the printer. This required another hour to fix! It took two-and-a-half hours to do a five-minute job! If I had known everything involved, I never would have bothered.

Breaking Off Communication

On a similar note, I recently approached God with a simple question, but as I prayed my heart accused me. I wasn't on speaking terms with Him. I had broken off communication because He was dealing with me about something I wasn't ready to give up. I felt guilty, walking in disobedience. Instead of waving the white flag of surrender, I wrestled with God. I knew that to restore fellowship with Him, I needed to first resolve this conflict.

Like copying the tape, the simple act of talking with the Lord was turning into a major issue. All I wanted was a quick answer about something unrelated.

I sometimes wonder how many other Christians are not on speaking terms with God because they have something in their lives they don't want to give up. The simplest act of saying "good morning" to the Lord seems impossible. If there is an unwillingness to restore fellowship (involving surrender, repentance and forgiveness), there is a sense of shame and guilt. We may think He won't talk to us about anything else until we resolve this area. Or we may feel that He has shut us out.

The thought of everything involved in talking to God is exhausting when our fellowship with Him is broken. Not talking with Him seems easier than restoring fellowship. If we do this long enough, we live a life of not hearing God's voice.

Restoring Communication

Thankfully, God is gracious. Relinquishing what has separated us from the Lord is best. As we give in, heartfelt sorrow replaces stubbornness. He is abundant in mercy and will forgive us despite what we have done.

> *If we confess our sins, he is faithful and just and will forgive us our sins and purify us from all unrighteousness (1 John 1:9).*

If we are too weak to give up our sin, He can strengthen us.

> *I can do everything through him who gives me strength (Phil. 4:13).*

If we love our sin, He is willing to change our desires as we surrender our heart to Him. Regardless of what we need for restoration, God will provide it.

> *His divine power has given us everything we need for life and godliness through our knowledge of him who called us by his own glory and goodness. Through these he has given us his very great and precious promises, so that through them you may participate in the divine nature and escape the corruption in the world caused by evil desires (2 Pet. 1:3-4).*

God provides everything we need, except our will. We must decide to say "yes" to God and surrender to Him. He will even cleanse our consciences.

Let us draw near to God with a sincere heart in full assurance of faith, having our hearts sprinkled to cleanse us from a guilty conscience (Heb. 10:22).

A clean conscience frees us to talk with God. Whether we have a simple question or a greater need, we have restored communication.

God Talks With Sinful People

Sometimes we need to talk to God before we can turn from sin. We may need to know the key to our bondage or addiction before we can be free. We may need His encouragement to surrender. God allows us, even encourages us, to talk with Him before we turn from our sin.

Scripture has many examples of God talking with a sinful person. He spoke with Adam when he was hiding his nakedness. Adam was guilty of the original sin, but before God forgave him He called out, "Adam, where are you?" They had a conversation while Adam was unforgiven. (Gen. 3:9-21)

Cain was the first murderer out of all mankind. He killed his brother, Abel, and God came looking for him. When asked about Abel's whereabouts, Cain said, "Am I my brother's keeper?" Again, a conversation followed between God and a sinful man not yet forgiven or even repentant. (Gen. 4:9-15)

God spoke to Egypt's heathen pharaoh and told him not to touch Abraham's wife, Sarah[64]. In a dream God spoke to Pontius Pilate's wife concerning Jesus. She was a Roman and there is no evidence she was a Jew keeping the commandments.

Every Christian talked to God before they became a Christian. The Bible says God will save everyone who calls upon the name of the Lord. This means that before God saved us, we had to call out to Him. We know that God also talked to each of us while we were sinners. In John 6:44, Jesus says that no one comes to Him unless the Father draws him[65]. That means God communicated with each of us while we were still sinners and drew us to Jesus. There is ample precedent for God talking with sinful people and vice versa.

God Will Give You What You Need to Restore Communication

God has given us the privilege of talking with Him even when we are living in sin or disobedience. Obviously, He wants us to live a life of obedience, but this is not a requirement for talking with Him. Even when we feel like we have a major issue to get right before we can have the simplest conversation with God, He will talk to us anyway.

Forget hauling out the stereo, connecting the speakers, fixing the labels and hooking up the printer. Allow yourself to talk to Him even when you feel guilty, unclean or disobedient. If you let Him, He will talk to you. He wants to take you by the hand and lead you into the life you should be leading. He will even give you everything you need.

His divine power has given us everything we need for life and godliness through our knowledge of him who called us by his own glory and goodness. Through these he has given us his very great and precious promises, so that through them you may participate in the divine nature and escape the corruption in the world caused by evil desires (2 Pet. 1:3-4).

All you have to do is be willing and start a conversation. Chances are He has already been speaking to you!

23 Are You Good Enough to Hear?

What more could a Little Leaguer ask for—a baseball coach who used to play professional ball! When I moved up from the minor league to the majors in Little League, the older players intimidated me. I often struck out without ever taking the bat off my shoulder. I wasn't a very good player.

Then Jerry came along. He was a retired pitcher for the Houston Astros and our entire league was in awe of him. Jerry came to coach our team and we just knew we would win the championship that year.

I remember our catcher begging Jerry to pitch to him. The catcher was big for his age, and seemed to think he was stronger still. Jerry had more "heat" than our catcher could ever hope to handle, but finally agreed. Our coach took the pitcher's mound and started slowly warming his arm and gauging the catcher's ability. The catcher kept pestering Jerry for faster and harder pitches.

We thought he was hurling pitches a thousand miles an hour, though I now realize he never threw as fast as he could. The catcher fell silent as he tried to catch like a professional. Then he chided for a fastball. Jerry probably tossed him an easy one, but to us it was smoke. It rocked the catcher back on his heels and left him shaking his hand like it was on fire. We witnessed the fastest pitch that small ball park had ever known. The catcher's constant banter halted as he pulled off his glove to examined his hand. When he next spoke, it wasn't with the same playful harassment. It was a speech of Jerry's pitching prowess and he told anyone who would listen. I don't remember Jerry pitching to him ever again.

I played second base, or should I say that I was a second baseman, for I rarely played in a game. I was second string. Under Jerry's tutelage, I steadily improved. During a pre-game practice in the middle of the season, Jerry turned to me and said "I want you to start at second base tonight." I couldn't believe it. Every player dreams of being a starter and now I had my chance. Immediately the excitement evaporated in the presence of self-doubt.

I looked at the coach and said, "I'm not good enough, let Mark start." It was then that this former pro said, "I know more about baseball than you do. I say you're good enough to start." That's all I needed to hear. He knows a lot more than I do, I thought. If he says I'm good enough then I am! That one comment and all it represented stayed with me through the years.

During my last season in Little League, I was the regular starting second basemen. In one game the opposing team had a runner on first and another on third. Often in this situation, the runner on first will steal second at the first opportunity. If the catcher tries to throw him out, the runner on third steals home, gaining a valuable run.

So I wasn't surprised when the runner on first began to steal second. Only he started too soon—before the pitcher threw the pitch. The pitcher, seeing the steal, turned and threw the ball to me. The runner on third ran for home. It all happened so fast I barely had time to think—I just reacted. I tagged out the runner coming from first, and then threw the ball home as hard as I could. Like a fastball pitch from second base, the throw was a perfect strike, enabling the catcher to tag the third-base runner.

We just made a double play! Our team went wild. The fans were cheering in the stands. The opposing team's coach was chewing out the third-base runner. I stood there dumbfounded and couldn't believe what the pitcher had done. As I stared at him in amazement, he gave me a mischievous grin.

Moments like that are what memories are made of. It's one of my most cherished childhood recollections, watching all those kids and adults cheer me on. All because Jerry had told me I was good enough.

God's children sometimes feel they're not good enough to hear His voice. The pastor and the televangelist can hear from God, but we can't because we're not good enough. Maybe we think our sin is too great or our life is too lowly. We figure it's because we haven't done anything special for Him. We feel unworthy to ask, or even to hope, that God would speak to us. Like my experience in baseball, low self-esteem makes a person unwilling to even try to hear from God.

Am I Good Enough?

God's answer is to give us His righteousness. Not that we deserve anything from God, for if we depend on our own merit and goodness, we will fall short. No one can earn the privilege of hearing God's voice. No one, that is, except Jesus. He led a perfect life then died for our imperfection. He offers us the best deal we will ever encounter: His life in exchange for our death. He offers us His righteousness for our wretchedness. This is the message of salvation[66].

Our Righteousness Comes From Christ

It doesn't matter how this lie affects us. The answer is always the same: Christ gives His righteousness to us freely. We are not worthy. We can do nothing by ourselves to earn God's approval or favor. No amount of good deeds can make us worthy. In this world some people seem much better than others. Perhaps they have integrity, respect others, love their fellow man, help the needy, and do things that we consider noble. Even they are not good enough. Wise King Solomon knew this:

There is not a righteous man on earth who does what is right and never sins (Eccl. 7:20).

The Apostle Paul said:

For all have sinned and fall short of the glory of God (Rom. 3:23).

And:

I know that nothing good lives in me, that is, in my sinful nature. For I have the desire to do what is good, but I cannot carry it out. (Rom. 7:18).

The Apostle John was blunt about it:

If we claim to be without sin, we deceive ourselves and the truth is not in us (1 John 1:8).

Even "good" people aren't good enough to please God. They may seem to be "better" than others, but for all their good works, no one can attain God's standard of perfection.

When we receive Christ as our Savior, He grants us His righteousness. His is perfect and righteous:

> *He is the Rock, his works are perfect, and all his ways are just. A faithful God who does no wrong, upright and just is he (Deut. 32:4).*

And He gives His righteousness to us:

> *And I [Paul] be found in him [Christ], not having a righteousness of my own that comes from the law, but that which is through faith in Christ-the righteousness that comes from God and is by faith (Phil 3:9 brackets mine).*

God considers us as righteous as His Son because Christ gave us His righteousness. This is how we get into heaven.

We Receive Righteousness, We Don't Earn It

If the righteousness Christ freely gave to us isn't enough, what more must we do to add to His work on Calvary? What must we add to improve upon the blood of Jesus for our redemption? Nothing! He did it all for us! This means that when we surrendered our life to Him, He gave us His righteousness. "That's too easy," you say. Yes, easy for us, but it cost Him everything. This is the wonder of Jesus' love. He gave His life for us so we could freely receive everything He has for us.

It is incredibly easy because of Him. We simply receive what He has to give. We don't have to earn it—we couldn't if we tried. He has given us the ability to hear His voice and we don't have to earn the right to hear it. He already made us righteous.

Receive His Righteousness Now

If you have not accepted Jesus Christ as your savior, do it now. Receive His free gift of righteousness. Exchange your sin for His life. Turn to the appendix now and learn how to become a Christian. Accept Christ as your savior and open your heart to hear His voice. He has already been calling you. Now is the time to answer.

We Are Good Enough to Hear His Voice

As you seek an attitude of prayer and seek God's face, listen to Him say to you, "I know more about righteousness than you do and you are good enough to hear My voice."

24   What God Talks About

I was getting a bad case of heartburn as I munched on a basketful of chips in a Mexican restaurant—and it wasn't from the salsa!

It was during my Bible college days and a buddy and I were having a late lunch. He was telling me all the delicate details of a mutual friend's secret. I was trying to be patient because I urgently needed his advice about my own private matter. Then it hit me—this guy might not be the best steward of my private thoughts. If he spoke so freely about our other friend's confidence, what's to keep him from revealing the troubling details of my own love life?

I learned a valuable lesson that day and have been spared pain and embarrassment by using the following criteria. When deciding whether to confide in someone, always consider what they have told you about others. Have they spoken of the secrets of others? Have they been a faithful confidant?

Gossip is More Than Lies and Half-Truths

I used to think gossip and rumors consisted of lies and half-truths until one of my instructors opened my eyes with this definition of gossip:

Gossip is talking about something when you are not part of the problem or part of the solution.

How simple and clear! Notice that according to this definition, gossip has nothing to do with truth. We shouldn't discuss the personal matters of others when it is out of our realm of involvement—

despite how truthful it may be. At first this principle seemed too narrow. But the more I have pondered it over the past twenty years, the more I agree with it.

God Doesn't Gossip

God hates gossip and never engages in it. What freedom! We have complete liberty and confidence in being transparent with Him because He is a faithful and trustworthy Confidant. We can confide in Him with assurance that He won't divulge privileged information unless it is in our best interest.

In the Bible God revealed to the world and the ages David's sin with Bathsheba. Doesn't this show that God will talk about our sins, problems and secrets? Scripture sometimes reveals people's failures that they, no doubt, would prefer He didn't. His motive for disclosure is for our benefit. He exposes sinful nature and reveals the potential we all have for evil. It also displays God's mercy, love and forgiveness. God doesn't reveal them recklessly, thoughtlessly or in gossip. Consider the large number of people mentioned in the Bible and the vast number of sins their lives represent. The few recorded is a testimony to God's discretion. He is the perfect, trustworthy Confidant!

Gossip Relates to Hearing God's Voice

How does this relate to hearing God's voice? When God speaks to us, it will be about things that concern us. He won't reveal other people's sins to us unless we are part of the problem or part of the solution. This wonderful principle shows us where to focus our "hearing." Rather than looking into the lives of others to discern their sin or investigate their faults, we should concentrate on God's dealings in our lives.

Beware!

When we find ourselves on the lookout for the sordid details of people's sins, beware! If someone is proud of their "discernment" as they expose the faults of others, beware! Some use the voice of the Lord as their conduit of smut. With religious overtones they may say, "God showed me that the deacon has a problem with lust" or that, "The pastor's wife has a spirit of Jezebel." They spiritualize their own sin of gossip by purveying in the sins of others. They speak to justify and validate their own evil heart by claiming "God told me."

The issue here is not whether they got their information from God.

The issue is why they seek to harm and why they fail to act in the best interest of their brother or sister in Christ.

Though some may call it "discernment," God views gossip as sin:

There are six things the LORD hates, seven that are detestable to him...a false witness who pours out lies and a man who stirs up dissension among brothers (Prov. 6:16, 19).

The Apostle Paul was aware of this sin:

We hear that some among you are idle. They are not busy; they are busybodies (2 Thess. 3:11).

Besides, they get into the habit of being idle and going about from house to house. And not only do they become idlers, but also gossips and busybodies, saying things they ought not to (1 Tim. 5:13).

Those who "spiritualize" gossip make it appear acceptable, perhaps even virtuous. They present it with redeeming qualities, calling it discernment, insight, even revelation and then add a short postscript, "Please pray for them." All of this is done with a great display of spirituality.

They do not fool God and we shouldn't let them fool us either:

and slander your own mother's son. These things you have done and I kept silent; you thought I was altogether like you (Ps. 50:20-21).

God doesn't speak about people's sin without reason. He isn't like the busybody who gossips, but portrays it as spirituality. Neither will He ignore this sin.

But I will rebuke you and accuse you to your face (Ps. 50:21).

Be mindful of What You Say

To avoid the sin of gossip, the wise person carefully considers what they say. Jesus reminds us that we will answer to Him:

But I tell you that men will have to give account on the day of judgment for every careless word they have spoken (Matt. 12:36).

He also encourages us to first judge ourselves:

Do not judge, or you too will be judged. For in the same way you judge others, you will be judged, and with the measure you use, it will be measured to you. Why do you look at the speck of sawdust in your brother's eye and pay no attention to the plank in your own eye? (Matt. 7:1-3).

God's admonitions strengthen the sincere heart. It recognizes the seriousness of gossip and prompts us to guard our tongue. It also stands watch over the ears, protecting them from the idle talk of others.

...And if God Speaks to us About Another?

How should we respond when the Lord speaks to us about someone? What should we do if our genuine gift of discernment, insight or revelation perceives the sin of another?

Many years ago the leaders of our ministry gathered to consider the moral failure of a prominent minister, which had recently became public. Though we discussed the man and his sin for hours, we refrained from gossip. Our purpose was to consider ourselves. We reminded each other that "there, but for the grace of God, go I". The Apostle Paul endorses using others' sins as an opportunity for self-reflection:

> Brothers, if someone is caught in a sin, you who are spiritual should restore him gently. But watch yourself, or you also may be tempted (Gal. 6:1).

God may use the sin of another to turn our sights inward. He may speak to us about them, not to gossip, but to admonish us. David's sin with Bathsheba instructs us in the evils of sin. Sampson's story warns us about worldliness. Korah's saga cautions against rebellion.

At other times, God may speak to us about others so that we can be part of the solution. He may call upon us to pray, counsel or instruct them. We may use it as an opportunity to instruct our children or seek advice from our elders. In this context, it is not gossip, but being part of the solution either for them or ourselves.

A Rule of Thumb

Are we safe in hearing from God? Should we be concerned about using discernment, insight or revelation? A good rule of thumb is that God will speak to us in areas of our responsibility. He will speak to us about our own lives. He will speak to the businesswomen about her work responsibilities and the family man about his children. He will speak to pastors about their congregations. These are all legitimate areas we should seek to hear from the Lord about, because they are part of our authority. We can even ask the Lord to share with us anything He wishes, as an example to us.

God loves the person we see fault in and wants to restore them, but He won't gossip about them to you. If He chooses to speak to us about them, we must maturely consider the great responsibility this entails. Our heart, like His heart, should reach out in love. We must be very careful to protect His trust in us and pursue His purposes for them. We should respond as Jesus would.

As good stewards of what others tell us, we must take great care that we handle it rightly. We should never find ourselves munching chips and salsa while we gossip about the lives of others.

25 Making Sense of What You Hear

While ministering overseas in the early 1990s I met a successful Christian businessman. I was in Asia talking to audiences about hearing God's voice in business and how the Lord wants to speak to us in this area of our lives. This man became very enthusiastic about the teaching and wanted to fly me to his country the next week and talk with some of his Christian friends about it.

When I arrived, he told me about several business opportunities he was considering. One in particular was a joint venture and involved more than $300 million. I asked the Lord about it and He said "yes." The man readily received this and went forward with the project. He was a wonderful, devoted man of God, who happened to be wealthy. He seemed much more interested in serving the Lord than in money. It was a joy to meet someone who had their priorities in order. I ended up staying in his home for several days and got to know his wife and his parents.

I heard from him again several years later. He called to ask me to pray about several business situations he was considering. We proceeded to review the dozen or so different projects and investment opportunities over the phone. I was a bit overwhelmed by the number of projects we were discussing and the huge amounts of money involved. Even so, with each proposition he presented, I sensed a distinct "no" in my spirit.

I didn't tell him what I felt God was saying—that he should either get his money out or not get involved. I wanted to wait and hear everything he was considering before I responded.

By the end of our discussion, I had hit overload and felt as if my ability to hear from God was crashing down around me. Why did I feel so negative about every single proposition? The guy had to invest his money somewhere, didn't he? He couldn't stuff it in a mattress. Afraid to say what I had heard and not wanting to be responsible for investing this amount of money, I told him I would pray about it and call him back. I never did.

Before continuing, let me make it clear that I don't believe God is interested in speaking to us as a spiritual get-rich-quick scheme. Neither do I believe that a businessperson needs a cadre of people who hear from God to manage their business affairs. However, I do believe God would like to speak to His people about every area of their lives, including money and business. Purity of heart, integrity, and biblical principles are vital in this area, as they are in other areas of our life.

This phone call left me reeling. Why did it happen this way? I had heard from God in the past for prominent people and in business matters, some of them representing large amounts of money. If I were hearing accurately, it didn't make sense why God was telling him no about everything.

Within six months of this phone call, Asian economies took a turn for the worse. It began in Thailand and spread throughout Asia. Indonesia was hit hard. Riots broke out. President Suharto stepped down. Indonesia still has not recovered economically.

I think back on what I heard from the Lord and now it all makes sense. God was telling this man to get his money out of Indonesia. If he had invested in the U.S. or other stable markets, he would have been all right. I can only guess at what may have happened to him. As of this writing, I still have not talked with him. I repented to God for not telling him what I heard. I clammed up and it may have cost him a great deal of money, not to mention what may have happened to his faith in God. I can only hope and pray that he too heard from God and obeyed. Perhaps he weathered the storm and with God's guidance came out on top.

God Doesn't Always Make Sense

I reacted in this situation by feeling that I was not hearing correctly. What I should have done was to tell the man exactly what I was hearing and leave the matter with him and God to work out.

Over the years I have noticed that many people expect to have an inner witness when God speaks. They want to have a sense of confirmation or agreement within themselves that it is God speaking to them. When this doesn't happen, the common reaction is to doubt they are hearing accurately. In those cases, we need to just accept that it is God and realize that His voice and His direction doesn't always have to make sense.

God Didn't Always Make Sense to Those in The Bible

The Bible has many examples of God's words not making sense to the reader. Until the time of Christ, the Jews struggled with contradictory Old Testament prophecies. Some prophesies said the Messiah would be a suffering Servant while others portrayed Him as a conquering King.

Christians now understand that some of these point to Jesus' first coming while others point to His second coming. When Jesus was on earth, He sometimes spoke in confusing, obscure ways that confused His listeners. When confronted about it by His disciples, He explained that He was doing it on purpose so that people wouldn't understand.

The disciples came to him and asked, "Why do you speak to the people in parables?" He replied, "The knowledge of the secrets of the kingdom of heaven has been given to you, but not to them. This is why I speak to them in parables: Though seeing, they do not see; though hearing, they do not hear or understand." (Matt. 13:10-11,13).

In this instance, God's words didn't make sense to people because He didn't want them to understand. There are other times when God wants us to comprehend, but we misunderstand. This would have happened if it had been me, and not Abraham, to whom God revealed the covenant of circumcision. I'm sure I would have rebuked the devil and refused to believe it was God's voice, especially when considering that pagans practiced castration to show dedication to their gods.

How did Abraham know it was God telling him to do this and not the influences of his pagan surroundings? Abraham got it right. I'm not sure how many of us would have. It just doesn't make sense.

God is on a Higher Level

God thinks and acts on a higher level than we do:

As the heavens are higher than the earth, so are my ways higher than your ways and my thoughts than your thoughts (Is. 55:9).

Communication between these two levels can often be difficult. When a three-year-old asks where babies come from, explanations are often brief, shallow and inaccurate. They just can't understand until they get older. When we asked God about things we can't understand, He doesn't lie. As a result, His responses often don't make sense because we don't have the capacity to understand. In these situations I have found that God usually chooses not to answer the question we ask, but instead tells us what we need to know.

God Knows The Future

Still another instance when God's voice may not make sense is when He is speaking about the future. He may be only interested in our understanding when we reach that time. For example, the Jews did not understand the Old Testament prophecies at the time in which God gave them. In a similar way, look at what the Apostle John said concerning Jesus' triumphal entry into Jerusalem:

At first his disciples did not understand all this. Only after Jesus was glorified did they realize that these things had been written about him and that they had done these things to him (John 12:16).

God's voice may only make sense when our life catches up with the future.

We May Not Like What God Has To Say

Occasionally we may not want to acknowledge what God is saying simply because we don't like it. We can subconsciously, but intentionally, refuse to understand it so that we don't have to come to grips with it.

How Should We Respond?

What do we do when God speaks and it doesn't make sense? We should simply obey without requiring an explanation. Abraham obeyed God and was considered righteous by God as a result[69]. I should have obeyed and told the Indonesian man to take his money out of the business endeavors he was considering. Obedience, not omniscience, is what is important to God.

This is particularly true concerning following God's path for our life. As He leads us, God sometimes guides us by vision. He puts a dream in our heart for us to fulfill. We are to stay on track as we fulfill this vision. However, there are other times when life is like walking in the dark. We don't know where we are or where we are going. We ask God to turn on the lights, to show us what we are to do or where we are to go. Instead, God leaves the lights off and says, "Put your right foot forward and wait for further instructions."

When we are obedient, He says, "OK, now put your left foot forward." In this way, He's leading us, not by a vision, but by single steps. The course of our life may not make sense, but if we are obedient, we will get to our destination. Both vision and single steps are valid ways of being led by God. Most of us will alternate between the two. When we are led by vision, God's work in our life makes sense. When we are led by single steps, it often doesn't make sense.

Whatever the reason, sometimes God's words to us don't make sense. Neither confusion nor clarity is an indicator that it is God's voice, or the voice of another. Those with a heart of purity and obedience will often be the most successful at navigating these rapids.

26 A Matter of Responsiveness

I grew up in a cozy, rural neighborhood near Phoenix, Arizona, where many of our neighbors had horses, cows and chickens. It was a great place for kids and I had many wonderful adventures. We didn't have any horses, but my friend, Woody, did. How I loved helping Woody saddle up two of them to ride in the nearby open desert. One day Woody's parents brought home another horse—a gentle gelding that I got to ride while Woody rode his sleek, strong stud. I was a novice rider who could do little more than stay upright in the saddle, but I loved being around these strong animals capable of genuine affection. Woody, on the other hand, was an experienced rider who liked to ride fast.

True to his nature, as soon as we got to the desert, Woody spurred his horse into a hard gallop. I was happy to follow far behind in a gentle lope, but when my horse saw the stud running as hard as he could, he too began to gallop. Of the two horses and two riders, everyone was happy with this arrangement except me. I was bouncing in the saddle like a bicyclist peddling down a washboard road.

I had a few poor options. If I stayed on, my tailbone might be seriously injured. If I fell off, I might break something. Either way, I was in trouble. I yanked hard on the reins yelling, "Whoa!" The horse was either deaf or dumb, maybe both, and didn't seem to notice or care that I wanted him to stop. He ran as fast and hard as he could in pursuit of Woody and the stallion.

An obedient horse doesn't require severe reining, but with this horse I would have to use a lot of strength to rein him to turn—

something I was incapable of as a young, novice rider. Not only could I not stop the horse, but I couldn't guide him. He refused to turn and pursued Woody with reckless abandon. At this speed he could easily break a leg if he stepped in one of the many prairie dog holes.

My only recourse was to hold on for dear life to the saddle horn and ride it out. My cries of desperation got lost in the wind. Finally Woody stopped and turned back toward us. Only then did my horse slow to a trot. When we caught up, I renamed both my friend and my horse with several choice expletives (this was before I was a Christian).

Woody couldn't understand what the problem was. He didn't know my horse would not obey my commands. Not until later did we discover that rough handling by his previous owner had made my horse unresponsive to the bit in his mouth. I could have pulled on the reins all day and it wouldn't have made any difference to that otherwise gentle horse. The slightest desire on my part to turn or stop involved a huge amount of effort. Since the simplest commands were exhausting, anything elaborate was out of the question. I lost all interest in riding that particular horse.

We, too, can be unresponsive to the One who holds the reins of our life. Like the horse, we may not be rebellious, we may just be insensitive. The Lord may rein us gently and we don't even notice it. He may whisper and we don't hear it. Insensitivity isn't always the result of rebellion or self-will. Sometimes it's because we haven't taken the time to cultivate a hearing ear and a sensitive heart.

The horse's problem came from rough reining. In a similar way, if we subject our sensitive ears to rough treatment, they too will become insensitive. If God speaks to us and we disobey, we are subjecting our spiritual senses to friction with His will. If God whispers to us to do an act of service and we choose not to, our senses are further calloused. If we live a lifestyle subjecting our spiritual senses to the harshness of disobedience and unresponsiveness, we will lose sensitivity to the voice of the Lord. We will be like the runaway horse who can't respond to its rider's instructions, directions and warnings.

My horse caught sight of the running stallion and immediately took off after it. If we see someone sprinting after the will of God, it may inspire us. We may follow even if it is not God's direction for us. Like the gelding racing after the stallion, no amount of urging from God may get through to us to stop or to turn. It's just a matter of time until we step in a hole and get hurt. In our pain we accuse God of not watching over us, of not providing for us, or of not taking care of us. In reality, He was doing all of those things, we just wouldn't respond.

Responsiveness to the Lord

Driving a sports car is at the other end of the spectrum. A mere thought is translated into a command and the car responds effortlessly. The car's performance urges the driver to try faster starts and tighter turns. Taking a spin in a responsive car is a delight, but riding a hardened horse is torture.

When we become sensitive to the voice of God, His slightest commands result in our obedience. He can use us in ways He would have never before considered. Perhaps He has called you to lead others into salvation, heal the sick, or move in the miraculous. Your sensitivity and responsiveness to Him is essential to your effectiveness.

Three Simple Keys will help you be responsive to God's voice.

1.) Attentiveness: A first-time mother is acutely aware of her newborn's every sound and is responsive to their every need. The wide-eyed innocence of a young child hangs on every word of the beloved father. We should cherish everything God says. Our attitude should be like that of the Apostle Peter's:

"You do not want to leave too, do you?" Jesus asked the Twelve. Simon Peter answered him, "Lord, to whom shall we go? You have the words of eternal life" (John 6:67-68).

When we place supreme value on what God has to say, we will be quick to hear it. His words should thunder in our ears by virtue of their value and importance. We should hang on God's every word as He rivets our attention.

We should be more attentive than the accused listening to the judge . . .

more than the businessperson listening to the consultant . . .

more than the sick listening to the doctor . . .

more than the parent listening for their lost child.

When we realize that God's words are the most important we will ever hear, we will listen attentively to Him. We should stir up our desire to listen for and hear His voice.

Since, then, you have been raised with Christ, set your hearts on things above, where Christ is seated at the right hand of God. Set your minds on things above, not on earthly things (Col 3:1-2).

Now devote your heart and soul to seeking the LORD your God (1 Chr. 22:19).

This goes beyond realizing the importance of God's words. It deals with our passion, or lack of it, for hearing God. Like the lover who longs to hear the voice of his beloved, we should long for the voice of God.

My dove in the clefts of the rock, in the hiding places on the mountainside, show me your face, let me hear your voice; for your voice is sweet, and your face is lovely (Song 2:14).

Finally, we must take the initiative. Instead of waiting to be spoken to, we can initiate the conversation. We can take the first step and begin communicating with the Lord. This takes us out of a passive, waiting posture and puts us in an active, initiating stance.

When we value God's words to us, when we want to hear from Him, and when we take the initiative, we will become attentive to His voice.

2.) Obedience: Another key is obedience. Here is a spiritual phenomenon to grab hold of and remember: Obedience sharpens our hearing. When we disobey, our hearing is dulled. This undoubtedly relates to our will and desires. Our disobedience shows we don't want to hear and it affects our hearing.

The reciprocal is also true. When we obey, it improves our hearing. When God speaks to you, obey without rationalization or excuses. Obey without question. Obey without delay.

3.) Joy: Taking joy in hearing from God is also important. It takes time, energy and effort to pray and listen. If we view it as a chore, we can easily become weary in well-doing and lose the joy of hearing from God. Joy can result from realizing the miraculous nature of hearing God's voice.

Put these keys to practice in your life and feel the result of heightened sensitivity to God's voice. Sometimes it happens quickly. Paying attention, obeying and being joyful about it can dramatically affect our sensitivity to God's voice.

Like the pauper speaking to the prime minister, it is an honor to have the attention of Almighty God. He doesn't limit Himself to a word or two before moving onto more important people or things. He takes all the time we need and lavishes His attention on us.

The miracle of it! In the privacy of our hearts we can talk to God without uttering words. Our prayers reach across the great divide between natural and spiritual. Our messages are never carried astray or lost in the mail. He hears us every time!

27 When God Doesn't Speak

When I proposed to Mary, I was prepared for a "yes,"
"no," and even an "I don't know." I was prepared for
every answer, but the one I got.

Mary and I had been good friends for more than five years and best
friends for two of those years. Upon graduating from Bible college,
we moved back to our respective homes in different states only to be
reunited the next year when I moved to Florida. It was then that I
was smitten. I knew this was the woman God had chosen for me and
I was fairly certain she felt the same way about me. After months of
prayer and counsel, I decided to ask her to marry me.

I was sure she would accept, but I didn't want to take anything for
granted so I prepared myself for the possibility that she might say no.
I even considered that she might want to think about it. When I was
as prepared as I could be, I planned my proposal.

The big day arrived and I took Mary to a beautiful local park where
I spread out a blanket and put a Christian tape in the boom box. I
asked her to close her eyes as I retrieved a carefully written proposal
from my pocket and read it to her. I told her all the reasons I respect-
ed and admired her. I recounted her virtues and spoke of her wonderful qualities. I read slowly, allowing her to bask in the warmth of
the words. With her eyes still closed, I finished reading by asking her
to be my wife.

Her eyes popped open in amazement. She didn't move, didn't
speak—nothing. A million thoughts raced through my mind. My
heart leaped into my throat where its pounding threatened to choke

me. The moment stretched into an eternity as I searched her face for a response. She looks excited, that's good, I told myself, trying to bolster my courage.

Her eyes were wide open in surprise, she seemed frozen in time. I wasn't prepared for shocked silence. I agonized as the seconds ticked by. She didn't eagerly embrace me like a woman who has just met her Prince Charming riding on a white horse. Had I misjudged her? Was I only moments away from devastation?

I couldn't stand the silence any longer. I had to ask again. "Well?" I finally blurted out.

Her eyes, which had been staring blankly ahead, focused on me. She awakened from her reverie with a start. She blurted back, "Well, yes!" Oh happy day! The jumble of emotions of fear, confidence and uncertainty were washed away by elation. The woman of my dreams had agreed to be my wife!

Sometimes God is Silent

Most Christians experience times when they desperately need to hear from God. Like my marriage proposal, they ask something very important and are prepared for however God might answer. What they may not be prepared for is silence, which can be very unsettling.

We may think we are unable to hear and that is why God seems silent. If the question is charged with emotion, we may even become angry with the Lord for not answering. If we urgently need an answer, we may be filled with worry and stress as we petition God to speak to us.

Our ideas for making God speak are endless. We may pray more often or longer, thinking it will cause God to break His silence. We may fast or read His Word, trying to get an answer. We may even suspect that demonic interference is blocking His message from getting to us[70]. We may spend endless amounts of time and energy trying to figure out what God is saying and why we aren't hearing His answer. This chapter has some keys to understanding those times when God is silent.

God Loves to Communicate

God loves to talk. He is a Communicator and enjoys speaking to us. Speech and communication from God play a big part in the Bible. In the beginning God created by speaking. After making man, we find Him in the Garden talking with Adam and Eve. After they sinned, He spoke to them, along with the serpent, about their punishment. In fact, the Bible itself is God communicating with mankind.

God spoke directly with Adam and Eve until sin dulled the human ear. With this obstacle in place, God remained committed to communicating with us. He used many different means to get through to us: such as angels, prophets, Scripture, signs and wonders, dreams, visions, trances, and Jesus Himself. Jesus then sent the Holy Spirit to lead and guide us. We might say that God bent over backwards to maintain communication with us.

In his book *Hearing God*[1] author Dallas Willard points out six ways God addressed people within the Bible: a phenomenon plus a voice, a supernatural messenger or an angel, dreams and visions, an audible voice, the human voice, and the human spirit or the still, small voice.

God certainly goes the extra mile to get through to us. Yet even in light of all He has done, we still sometimes hear silence when we talk with God.

There is an Exception to Every Rule

God wants to communicate, but there are times when He doesn't speak. Understanding some reasons He may be silent can aid us in restoring communication.

Silent About One Thing, But Speaking About Another

There are times when God may want to talk with us about one area of our life, but we want to talk about something else. We're so insistent at what we want to talk about that we overlook everything else. We can focus to the point of having tunnel vision, even obsessing over a question or an issue. When we become so immersed in our concern that we forget everything else, we may feel as if God is silent.

In truth, He may be talking, but about something of concern to Him. Perhaps it is something we aren't concerned about, or perhaps it pales in importance when compared with what's on our mind. We need to realize that God may feel the same way. He may be very concerned about what's on His mind and may not share our sense of urgency about our concern. This leaves us with the situation of Him talking about one thing while we're talking about another. Our course of action in this situation should be to turn our attention to God and discover what's on His mind.

Turning our attention away from our concerns and giving ourselves fully to the Lord helps us realize that God may be speaking
about something else. Something other than what we are praying
about. We hear silence when we are focused on an issue about which
God chooses not to talk. When we decide to talk about what is
important to Him, we may find that He has much to say to us.

God May Be Waiting For Our Obedience

There are times when God grows tired of repeatedly telling us the
same thing. Like a child who doesn't like the parent's answer, we
sometimes ask God the same question, hoping to get a different
answer. If we deeply object to His answer, we may deny we even
heard Him. Responding this way over time may cause God to stop
speaking about the issue. He's already answered us, His answer will
not change and He's tired of talking about it.

In this situation, God may grow silent. He may stop talking to us
when we have refused to obey because we don't like what He is saying. Even so, God waits patiently for us to turn away from what we
want and accept His decisions. Until we do, He may choose not to
say anything more.

God's ways are best. Even if we could talk God into an answer we
like, would this be wise? We need to honor God's decisions, deny
ourselves and trust Him. When we obey God and accept His decisions we will stop the behavior that results in His silence.

If disobedience or rejection of His answer is the reason for God's
silence, there is only one thing to do. Return to the last thing you
remember Him saying and make sure you were obedient. Return to
the place of departure from His will and obey.

If enough time has passed, you may have forgotten the last thing
He said. In this case, go back to the last point in your life where you
know with certainty you were obedient and start again from there. If
all else fails, prepare yourself to say "Yes" to whatever He might say
and ask Him what you should do. If He knows you are willing in
every way, He may very well respond with love and mercy and
instruct you again.

God Doesn't Talk During a Test

In her book *Dealing With Life's Challenges*[72] author Evelyn Hamon
says God doesn't talk to us when we are taking a test. She likens
God's work in our life to school. First, we hear the lesson and then
there is a test to find out if we learned what the teacher was trying to
teach us.

She compares this to the way God teaches us. In time, He will test us to see if we learned and if we are willing to put the lesson into practice. God tested Abraham when He told him to slay Isaac on the altar[73]. God tested the children of Israel by sending manna from heaven (Ex. 16:4). He used false prophets to test Israel[74].

During a test the teacher usually tells the student who has a question, "I'm sorry, but I can't answer questions during a test." Any other time the teacher will answer questions, but not during a test.

God may be silent with us when He tests us. He may allow us to face difficult circumstances to teach us to endure. Peter said:

Dear friends, do not be surprised at the painful trial you are suffering, as though something strange were happening to you (1 Pet. 4:12).

The Lord may orchestrate a situation as a proving ground to find out if we were paying attention to how He was dealing with us. Perhaps He's teaching us to love others. Perhaps it is patience, peace or trust that He's trying to work in our lives. At some point in time He will test us. He wants to know if we have learned and if we are willing to apply it in our life.

During these times of testing, God may be silent even though we barrage Him with questions and wonder, What test? I didn't know this was a test? Maybe we were totally unaware that God was trying to get through to us. Maybe we were playing hooky or goofing off. Sometimes Christians don't realize that God is always working in us . It catches them off guard.

But here's Evelyn Hamon's advice to those who "don't know the answer": Hand in your test paper. In other words, we can go to God and confess that we weren't paying attention. We can ask His forgiveness for not knowing the answers and turn in our test paper by asking Him to begin again.

The sooner we admit that we don't know the answer, the quicker the test will end and God will speak to us again. We may have to repeat the experiences He intended to instruct us. It is this process of teaching, testing, failing, and repeating the class that characterizes some Christians' lives. They continually repeat experiences.

We have even adopted the phrase of "going around the mountain again" to explain this process. One way to reduce this is to understand that God is working in us and that we should pay attention to the lesson. When we become attentive and learn, we can get out of this cycle and enter a positive cycle. Paul describes this in 2 Cor. 3:18:

And we, who with unveiled faces all reflect the Lord's glory, are being transformed into his likeness with ever-increasing glory, which comes from the Lord, who is the Spirit.

Be encouraged that the test isn't hard when you have learned—and know—the answers!

God Tests, But Never Tempts

God will test us to determine if we have learned, but He will never tempt us to do wrong. The Apostle James said:

When tempted, no one should say, "God is tempting me." For God cannot be tempted by evil, nor does he tempt anyone (James 1:13).

God will never entice us to sin. However, He will give us an opportunity to prove what we have learned. This is the difference between temptation and testing.

We May Not Be Ready to Hear

It seems like just yesterday when my little girl said, "Daddy, I know the doctor takes the baby out of Mommy's tummy, but how does it get in there?" I stumbled over a few words and then began to bluster, finally settling on "You aren't ready to hear. I'll tell you when you get older."

When she and our other children were older we used Larry Christianson's book *The Wonderful Way that Babies Are Made*[76] to explain this delicate yet crucial topic. Larry presents a healthy Christian perspective on human reproduction in a clear, but delicate manner. When our children were little, we told them only what they were ready to hear.

New Christians aren't ready to hear some things. Jesus said:

"Oh, there is so much more I want to tell you, but you can't understand it now" (John 16:12 TLB).

The implication in this verse is that Jesus had more things He wanted to say to them. But they were not ready, so He chose not to tell them.

There may be areas in your life where you cannot bear what Jesus has to say to you. The solution is to allow Him to do His perfect work in your life so that you can bear it. When He speaks to you, it will be with words of life, not of death. How ironic that we can bear up under the burden of the world and our flesh, but not the words of life.

Paul used the metaphor of weaning to illustrate how maturity determines the truth we are ready for:

I gave you milk, not solid food, for you were not yet ready for it. Indeed, you are still not ready (1 Cor. 3:2).

The writer of Hebrews puts it this way:

We have much to say about this, but it is hard to explain because you are slow to learn. In fact, though by this time you ought to be teachers, you need someone to teach you the elementary truths of God's word all over again. You need milk, not solid food! (Heb. 5:11-12)

Sometimes we may not be ready because of a lack of understanding. We don't understand algebra until we first master arithmetic. In other cases we may not be ready because we are unwilling to hear. How willing are we to hear that a deceased love one didn't make it to heaven? The thought can be traumatic, even torturous. Dealing with it may be easier if we don't speak about it.

In either case, whether we lack understanding or are unwilling to hear, there are times when God doesn't speak because we aren't ready to hear. In these times God may choose not to speak.

Perhaps God, in His mercy, withholds things from us so that we cannot wrestle with them. Jacob had a confrontation with God in the wilderness and wrestled with Him. God prevailed, but Jacob bore the scars of the contest for the rest of his life. How often has God avoided us? How often has He stepped aside when we came strutting down the road just to avoid a confrontation with us? How often has He not confronted us simply because to do so would result in greater harm than good?

Instead, He covers us by His blood and extends to us His mercy. Does this sound improbable? Does it sound contrary to the nature of God for Him to choose not to confront us with the truth?

Let's look at our own life. God may convict us of something we were blinded to. He may show us the darkness of our heart and begin to correct it. Yet how long did we harbor the issue before He spoke to us about it? It may have been months, years or even decades. During that time the Lord chose not to confront us with His truth because it wasn't time—it wouldn't have been best for us. This way, God causes mercy to triumph over judgment (James 2:13).

Accepting God's silence is sometimes wise. We can trust Him and surrender our need to know. There is a joy in the knowledge that God cares for us and will do what is best for us. When we are convinced of this, we don't need Him to explain every action He takes in our life. We learn to thank Him for His silence and mercy.

Taking the Next Step

What should you do when God is silent? The answer depends on why God is not speaking. As a handy summary to this chapter, here is a chart that suggests how we should respond to God, depending on why He is silent. It even has a recommendation when we don't know why.

GOD'S REASON FOR SILENCE	OUR RESPONSE
He is silent in one area, but speaking in another.	Focus on what God wants to talk about and place far greater importance on it than on what we prefer to talk about.
He is awaiting our obedience to something He already told us.	Surrender to God and be willing in anything He might ask.
He is testing us.	Admit we weren't paying attention, accept God's test "grade" and start over.
We aren't ready to hear because we lack understanding or willingness.	Grow in maturity a step at a time so that we become able to hear whatever He wishes to say to us. Develop trust in God so we don't feel the need to know.
We don't know why God is silent.	Be obedient and surrender to God's will. Ask Him to make clear anything you need to know. Enter His rest. Ask those you respect if they are aware of anything you are not.

Hear God's Voice with Clarity, Consistency & Confidence:

Experience is a wonderful teacher. It helps you to tell apart the twin voices of God and self. God may communicate with you by seeing, feeling, hearing, thinking, or a combination of these. As you discern between the voice of the Lord and the voice of your heart, God's voice will have clarity that will astonish you.

Hearing God's voice is more about developing a relationship than it is about gathering information. As we faithfully pursue an intimate relationship with Him, God will communicate with us consistently, with few exceptions.

Hearing God's voice is easy because we are created to communicate on His frequency. In the opening chapter I told how our baby monitor and our neighbor's cordless phone were on the same frequency, making it easy for us to hear her private phone conversation.

When we believe God's Word that "My sheep hear my voice," faith arises in our heart and we hear God's voice with confidence.

It doesn't matter if you are a beginner at hearing God's voice or a seasoned listener. There is a higher level you can come to in hearing from Him. My prayer is that the principles in this book will help you to hear God with greater clarity, consistency and confidence.

End Notes

1. American Heritage Dictionary; Houghton Mifflin Company; Boston. 1969

2. "The Post-it Note Story." Art Fry, the 3M engineer credited with inventing the Post-It Note, tells this story. The Post-it Note had its start in 3M's Central Research Department when Dr. Spence Silver was looking for ways to improve the acrylate adhesives used in many 3M tapes and in the medical, industrial and office markets. He was trying to make them stronger by experimenting with new materials in the molecule and by changing the way they were made. What followed was a classic case of serendipity, where you find something you are not looking for.

He had discovered an adhesive that formed itself into tiny spheres the diameter of a paper fiber. The spheres would not dissolve, could not be melted, and were very sticky individually. When they were coated onto tape backing, they would not stick very strongly, because the little spheres made intermittent contact between the tape backing and whatever you tried to stick them to, as compared to normal adhesives with smooth surfaces that make complete contact. He tried it again, and got the same result. It is always exciting for scientists to be able to duplicate their work.

Spence had discovered a new adhesive, but had no good idea of how to use it. If he had thrown it away, we all would have been the losers. Instead, he diligently told about his discovery to others in 3M who used adhesives. Fry went to one of his seminars and thought it interesting, but did not know how to use this new adhesive.

"I can remember the aggravation when it was time to stand up and sing in my church choir, only to find that the little piece of paper that I used to mark the music had fallen out, making me fumble about, trying to find the right page. This was followed by a dull sermon and my mind was wandering back to the music problem when I had one of those flashes of insight. Eureka! I think I could make a bookmark, using Dr. Silver's adhesive that would stick and remove without damaging the book."

The next day at work, Fry gathered paper and adhesive and prepared samples of the bookmark. He gave samples to his secretary, his supervisor, and other colleagues. They were pleased to get them, but after two weeks when asked if they wanted more, they said the bookmarks were working well, but they had not used all of the samples given them.

A short time later, Fry was writing a report and had a question about a piece of information. He attached a sample "bookmark" to the report with an arrow pointing to the information with a question on it. Bob Molenda, his manager at the time, wrote his answer on the bottom of the note and attached it to an item he was returning to me. It was during a coffee break the (sic) afternoon when both men realized that what they had was not just a "bookmark," but a new way to communicate and to organize information.

"Self-attaching Notes! Wow! We were very excited. My colleagues started using their bookmark samples as notes and soon were at my desk saying that they were instant addicts and demanding more samples. As the circle of addiction quickly spread within our product development laboratory, I came to the very exciting and satisfying realization that those little, self-attaching notes were a very useful product."

http://mustang.coled.umn.edu/inventing/Postit.html

3. Vulcanized rubber was accidentally discovered when Charles Goodyear observed natural rubber and sulfur together on a hot stove. Rubber for almost all ordinary purposes is vulcanized; exceptions are rubber cement, crepe-rubber soles, and adhesive tape. Vulcanized rubber is not sticky like raw rubber, does not harden with cold or soften much except with great heat, is elastic, springing back into shape when deformed instead of remaining deformed as unvulcanized rubber does, is highly resistant to abrasion and to gasoline and most chemicals, and is a good insulator against electricity and heat. The process of vulcanizing rubber by adding sulfur and heating was an incredibly useful, but an entirely unexpected discovery.

Potato chips were born near the turn of the previous century when a restaurant patron repeatedly asked the cook to make his fries more crunchy. The cook, in agitation, fried them to a crisp. The patron loved them and the potato chip became a favorite. This time the discovery was malevolent, but nonetheless accidental.

Silly Putty7, the popular child's toy, came into being in the 1940s when the U.S. War Production Board asked General Electric to synthesize a cheap substitute for rubber. James Wright, a company engineer assigned to the project in New Haven, Conn., developed a pliant compound dubbed "nutty putty" with no real advantages over synthetic rubber. In 1949, Paul Hodgson, a former advertising copywriter running a New Haven toy store, happened to witness a demonstration of the "nutty putty" at a party. He bought 21 pounds of the putty for $147, hired a Yale student to separate it into half-ounce balls, and marketed the putty inside colored plastic eggs as Silly Putty. When it outsold all other items in his store, Hodgson mass produced Silly Putty as "the toy with one moving part," selling up to 300 eggs a day.

Penicillin is another example of serendipitous discovery.

> Alexander Fleming had been working during and after World War I trying to find ways to kill bacteria isolated from infected wounds in order to find a way to treat wounds and prevent infections. Like most wars up to that time, infections of wounds rather than the wound itself caused the vast majority of deaths.

> When World War I was over, Fleming continued working at St. Mary's Hospital. One day in 1928, before tossing some old petri dishes of cul-

ture away, he made an accidental discovery of a blue mold growing on the culture of some harmful kind of bacteria. The mold seemed to be able to kill off the bacteria. A series of experiments later proved his findings and led to the discovery of penicillin. It was a strain of penicillia that could kill off bacteria while not causing any damage to wounds. It worked against many kinds of bacteria and was mostly safe for the human body.

Almost by accident, bacteriologist Alexander Fleming discovered that a green mould (sic) identified as Penicillium notatum would release a substance with the power to destroy bacteria. This discovery of the world's first antibiotic drug (Fleming named it Penicillin) created a new weapon against disease and opened the way for a revolution in medicine.

4. The incandescent light bulb is "a bulb containing a flammable substance, which is held in check by evacuating the oxygen, a current of electricity is passed through this carbonized filament and it glows but does not burn due to the lack of oxygen." (http://www.edisonnj.org/menlopark/incandescentlight.asp)

5. Spirit Filled Life Bible, Gen. Ed. Jack W. Hayford, Litt.D.; Thomas Nelson Publishers; See Word Wealth "Workmanship" Eph. 2:10.

6. "More than half the inhabitants of the world's oceans make their own light. From warm surface waters to the coldest darkest depths, these creatures use bioluminescence to hunt for food, find mates, and avoid predators. Since 99% of our biosphere is ocean, bioluminescence may be the most common form of communication on our planet. Marine Bioluminescence: Secret Lights of the Sea. Harbor Branch Oceanographic Marine Science Educational Series. http://shop.store.yahoo.com/hboigiftstore/marbiolsecli.html See also http://www.hboi.edu/

7. Pascho is a Greek word and means "to feel a sensation or impression." See Chapter 15 "Characteristics of Feeling" for an in-depth discussion of pascho.

8. Rev 2:7: "He who has an ear, let him hear what the Spirit says to the churches." To him who overcomes I will give to eat from the tree of life, which is in the midst of the Paradise of God."[1] (NKJ)

9. There are, of course, exceptions to this general principle. One such exception is when God is deliberately silent. Another is that those who have a reprobate mind will not hear.

10. 1 Kin. 19:3-4

11. 1 Kin. 19:3

12. 1 Kin. 19:4

13. Compare 1 Kin. 18:18, 21 & 45 with 1 Kin. 19:1-2.

14. The Sage Digital Library; John Wesley's Notes on the Whole Bible by John Wesley, SAGE Software Albany, OR, USA, Version 1.0 8 1996

15. 1 Kin. 18:13

16. New King James Version, Margin

17. John 16:13: "But when he, the Spirit of truth, comes, he will guide you into all

truth. He will not speak on his own; he will speak only what he hears, and he will tell you what is yet to come."

18. "God's Word, visions, dreams, angels, writing with His finger, rainbows, creation, a pillar of fire and a pillar of cloud, a consuming fire, supernatural signs, circumstances, the urim and thummim, and casting lots." Dawson, Joy. Forever Ruined for the Ordinary. Thomas Nelson Publishers, Nashville. Pg. 43.

19. The correlation between spiritual touch and the phrase "You should know His will" may seem strained, but this will be developed more completely later in this chapter.

20. See Chapter 8 "Inward Visions" for a detailed discussion on this pictorial language.

21. In Num. 23:3, Balaam instructs Balak to stay, but says he will "go" in hopes that God would meet with him. This indicates he sought a place of solitude so he could seek God and perhaps meet with Him.

22. His doctrine was false according to Rev. 2:14; and his practices were false according to 2 Pet. 2:15, Jude 1:11 and Num. 22-24.

23. He is identified as a soothsayer, or diviner, in Josh. 13:22.

24. See Num. 23:3.

25. When Jesus came to earth in the form of a man He emptied Himself of many of His divine qualities (Phil. 1:7). One of the things Jesus set aside was omniscience (all knowing), another was omnipresence (everywhere at once). Thus, Jesus didn't know about Nathanael, it had to be revealed to Him by the Father.

26. For more information, see "God Loves to Communicate" in Chapter 27 "When God Doesn't Speak."

27. See Chapter 1 "Hearing by Design" for a discussion on how we have been designed to receive from the Lord.

28. New Unger's Bible Dictionary; Moody Press of Chicago, Illinois. Copyright (C) 1988.

29. Nelson's Illustrated Bible Dictionary; Copyright (C) 1986, Thomas Nelson Publishers.

30. Matt. 10:5, 19-20, 27.

31. 1 Kin. 19.

32. Is. 30:21; Ezek. 3:12; 2 Kin. 7:5-7; Rev. 1:10.

33. The account of Paul's conversion is given in three places in the book of Acts (Chapter 9, 22 & 26). Paul says in Chapter 22 that his companions did not hear the voice (v. 9), while in Chapter 9 he says they did (v. 7). Matthew Henry's Commentary reconciles these passages, saying that they heard the sound of God's voice as a "confused noise," but did not understand what He said. (Matthew Henry's Commentary Acts 9:1-9 PP53)

34 John 12:28-30

35. "Dead Sea Scrolls"; Nelson's Illustrated Bible Dictionary, 1986, Thomas Nelson Publishers.

36. "Pilate, Pontius"; Nelson's Illustrated Bible Dictionary, 1986, Thomas Nelson

Publishers.

37. IBID

38. John 8:29, John 5:30, John 8: 28, John 9:4, John 12:49, John 14:10, John 14:20

39. "Witness of the Spirit"; New Unger's Bible Dictionary; originally published by Moody Press of Chicago, Illinois. 1988.

40. IBID

41. "Conscience"; New Unger's Bible Dictionary; originally published by Moody Press of Chicago, Illinois. 1988.

42. "Conscience"; International Standard Bible Encyclopedia, Electronic Database by Biblesoft, 1996.

43. Josh. 24:2: "And Joshua said to all the people, 'Thus says the Lord God of Israel: "Your fathers, including Terah, the father of Abraham and the father of Nahor, dwelt on the other side of the River in old times; and they served other gods.'" (NKJ)

44. "A...certain Jewish legends (e.g. Ber. Rab. 17) represent Terah as actually a maker of idols." "Terah" from International Standard Bible Encyclopedia, Electronic Database by Biblesoft, 1996.

45. The cutting of oneself during worship to attract the attention of the gods. This practice was strictly forbidden in ancient Israel: "You shall not cut yourselves nor shave the front of your head for the dead" (Lev. 19:28; 21:5; Deut. 14:1). "Cutting of the Flesh" from from Nelson's Illustrated Bible Dictionary), 1986, Thomas Nelson Publishers.

46. Matt. 14:14: "And when Jesus went out He saw a great multitude; and He was moved with compassion for them, and healed their sick." (NKJ)

47. Webster's New World Dictionary of the American Language, Uralic, David B. Ed., Warner Books, New York. 1984

48. Norman Simon, the Nobel laureate economist and cognitive scientist, has suggested that intuition is nothing more than the brain's capacity for subliminal computation. "Making Management Decisions: The Role of Intuition and Emotions," in Weston Agor (ed.), Intuition in Organizations. Newbury Park, CA: Sage Publication, 1989. Quoted from Intuition: A Link Between Psi and Spirituality by Jeffrey Mishlove, Director, Intuition Network at http://www.intuition.org/revision.htm

49. Col. 4:14 Luke the beloved physician and Demas greet you. (NKJ)

50. "Seem" from Vine's Expository Dictionary of Biblical Words 1985, Thomas Nelson Publishers.

51. Barnes' Notes, Electronic Database by Biblesoft, 1997.

52. Heb.10:16: "This is the covenant that I will make with them after those days, says the Lord: I will put My laws into their hearts, and in their minds I will write them." (NKJ)

Heb. 8:10: "For this is the covenant that I will make with the house of Israel after those days, says the Lord: I will put My laws in their mind and write them on their hearts; and I will be their God, and they shall be My people. (NKJ)

Eph. 1:18: "The eyes of your understanding being enlightened; that you may know what is the hope of His calling, what are the riches of the glory of His inheritance in the saints." (NKJ)

Luke 24:45: "And He opened their understanding, that they might comprehend the Scriptures." (NKJ)

I John 5:20: "And we know that the Son of God has come and has given us an understanding, that we may know Him who is true; and we are in Him who is true, in His Son Jesus Christ." This is the true God and eternal life." (NKJ)

2 Tim. 2:7: "Consider what I say, and may the Lord give you understanding in all things." (NKJ)

Matt. 13:11: "He answered and said to them, 'Because it has been given to you to know the mysteries of the kingdom of heaven, but to them it has not been given.'" (NKJ)

Eph. 3:18: "May be able to comprehend with all the saints what is the width and length and depth and height-." (NKJ)

53. Wind is a familiar emblem of the Spirit (Acts 2:2; Ezek. 37:9; John 3:8; 20:22) from Jamieson, Fausset, and Brown Commentary, Electronic Database by Biblesoft, 1997.

54. Chapman, Gary. The Five Love Languages, Moody Press, Chicago.

55. The Five Love Languages: Overview

Love Language No. 1: Words of Affirmation

Verbal compliments, or words of appreciation, are powerful communicators of love. They are best expressed in simple, straightforward statements of affirmation such as:

"You look sharp in that suit."

"Do you ever look nice in that dress! WOW!"

Encouragement requires empathy and seeing the world from your spouse's perspective. We must first learn to what is important to our spouse.

Love Language No. 2: Quality Time

A central aspect of quality time is togetherness. Two people sitting in the same room are in close proximity, but they are not necessarily together. Togetherness has to do with focused attention.

Quality time does not mean that we have to spend our together moments gazing into each others eyes. It means we are doing something together and we are giving our full attention to each other.

Love Language No. 3: Receiving Gifts

Gifts are visual symbols of love. Most wedding ceremonies include the giving and receiving of rings. The person performing the ceremony says, "These rings are outward and visible sings of an inward and spiritual bond that unites your two hearts in love that has no end." That is not meaningless rhetoric. It is verbalizing a significant truth--symbols have emotional value

Love Language No. 4: Acts of Service

Such actions as cooking a meal, setting a table, washing dishes, vacuuming, removing the white spots from the mirror, getting bugs off the windshield, taking out the garbage, changing the baby's diaper, painting a bedroom, dusting the bookcase, keeping the car in operating condition, cleaning the garage, mowing the grass, trimming the shrubs, raking the leaves, walking the dog, and changing the cat's litter box are all acts of service. They require thought, planning, time, effort, and energy. If done with a positive spirit, they are indeed expressions of love

Love Language No. 5: Physical Touch

Physical touch is also a powerful vehicle for communicating marital love. Holding hands, kissing, embracing, and sexual intercourse are all ways of communicating emotional love to one's spouse. For some individuals, physical touch is their primary love language. Without it, they feel unloved. With it, their emotional tank is filled and they secure in the love of their spouse.

(Excerpted from http://www.moodypress.org/promo/garychapman/LoveLanguages)

56. Please see Chapters 7-16 for more information on seeing, hearing and feeling

57. From "The Motivation Profile," ©2000, by Jay Arthur and Greg Engel, phone: 888-468-1537. Take the complete profile online at www.motivateeveryone.com.

58. See Chapter 1 for a complete discussion of how we are created and how this enables us to hear God's voice.

59. 2 Pet. 1:3-4

60. The Apostle Paul discussed this in the book of Romans. Romans 5 is about Adam's sin resulting in the sinful nature of all mankind. A key verse is 5:12. Chapter 6 explains that Christ overcame death. He gives us the power to overcome our sinful nature when we yield to Him (i.e. live according to God's will for us, obeying His commands and following His leading). A key verse is 6:11. Chapter 7 is Paul's vulnerable self-disclosure of how he struggled with his sin nature. Key verses are 7:18-19 Finally, Chapter 8 teaches that we can live victorious over the sin nature by the power of God. Key verse is 8:2.

61. Biblesoft's New Exhaustive Strong's Numbers and Concordance with Expanded Greek-Hebrew Dictionary. 1994, Biblesoft and International Bible Translators, Inc.

62. God shared His grief with Moses when the Israelites were in Egyptian bondage. Ex. 3:7-10: "The Lord said, 'I have indeed seen the misery of my people in Egypt. I have heard them crying out because of their slave drivers, and I am concerned about their suffering. So I have come down to rescue them from the hand of the Egyptians and to bring them up out of that land into a good and spacious land, a land flowing with milk and honey--the home of the Canaanites, Hittites, Amorites, Perizzites, Hivites and Jebusites. And now the cry of the Israelites has reached me, and I have seen the way the Egyptians are oppressing them. So now, go. I am sending you to Pharaoh to bring my people the Israelites out of Egypt.'" In this passage, God refers to hearing their cry and being concerned about their suffering. He shares His heart with Moses.

63. The ministry steps are adapted from the book Restoring the Foundations by Chester and Betsy Kylstra. It is available through

Proclaiming His Word Ministry, P.O. Box 2339, Santa Rosa Beach, FL 32459. Phone: 850-835-4060; online: www.phw.org

64. Pharaoh was sinful because he wasn't living according to the law of God given to the Jews and offering blood sacrifices as it prescribed.

65. John 6:44: "No one can come to me unless the Father who sent me draws him, and I will raise him up at the last day." (NIV)

66. If you have not dedicated your life to Christ and become a Christian, please take a few moments to read the Appendix.

67. Rom. 4:3-22 has a wonderful discussion of Abraham receiving God's righteousness through faith, not by works. This righteousness is also available to us through faith in Christ (Rom. 4:23-24). Eph. 2:8-9 tells us that this righteousness is available to us by grace through faith, not by our works.

68. George Whitefield (1714-1770), an 18th century clergyman, watching a condemned criminal being led to the execution chamber. As reported in Jim's Favorite Famous Quote, Quip, Axiom, and Maxim Repository. http://www.jimpoz.com/quotes/classics.asp

69. See Romans Chapter 4

70. In this instance, the Lord sent a message to Daniel, but demonic interference delayed it 21 days. Dan. 10:12-14: "Then he said to me, 'Do not fear, Daniel, for from the first day that you set your heart to understand, and to humble yourself before your God, your words were heard; and I have come because of your words. But the prince of the kingdom of Persia withstood me twenty-one days; and behold, Michael, one of the chief princes, came to help me, for I had been left alone there with the kings of Persia. Now I have come to make you understand what will happen to your people in the latter days, for the vision refers to many days yet to come.'" (NKJ)

71. Willard, Dallas. Hearing God: Developing a Conversational Relationship With God, InterVarsity press, Downers Grove, IL. Page 91.

72. Hamon, Evelyn. Dealing With Life's Challenges. Christian International Publishers; Santa Rosa Beach, FL.

73. Gen. 22, especially verses 1, 12.

74. Deut. 13:1-3: "If there arises among you a prophet or a dreamer of dreams, and he gives you a sign or a wonder, and the sign or the wonder comes to pass, of which he spoke to you, saying, 'Let us go after other gods'— which you have not known— ' and let us serve them,' you shall not listen to the words of that prophet or that dreamer of dreams, for the LORD your God is testing you."

(NKJ)

75. Phil. 2:13: "For it is God who is at work in you, both to will and to work for (His) good pleasure. (NAS)

76. Christianson, Larry. The Wonderful Way that Babies Are Made, Bethany House Publishers, Minneapolis, MN 1982.

Appendix

What is Salvation?

God is a loving Father.

Most of us have an image that the ideal father is someone who dearly loves his children and dotes on them—a man who is kind, patient and understanding. He is strong and protects his family. He desires the best for his children so he provides for them and prepares them for their future.

Well, this is the very nature of our Father in heaven. He is incredibly kind and loving. You can open up and share your heart Him, knowing that He completely understands and accepts you regardless of what you say or do. He responds with interest and compassion, giving you His undivided attention. His unconditional love for you is stronger than you can imagine. He wants the best for you and is eager to help, guide and protect you. He is the type of father we should want to run do, not run away from.

God desires only what is good for us.

God wants what's best for us and has never intended to harm us or make our life unpleasant. Lamentations 3:33 says:

For he does not willingly bring affliction or grief to the children of men.

Palms 119: 68 (TLB) says,

You (God) are good and do only good; make me follow your lead.

God is good and does only good things. He doesn't try to hurt us or grieve us. He is a wonderful Father who wants to draw His children close, love them, and have a wonderful relationship with them. He can be trusted.

The problem is sin.

As much as God wants to be close to us and take care of us, we are blocked from a wonderful relationship with Him because of sin. Sin came into the world through Adam and affects each and every one of us. No one escapes sin.

When Adam sinned, sin entered the entire human race. His sin spread death throughout all the world, so everything began to grow old and die, for all sinned (Rom. 5:12 TLB).

In Romans 3:23, Paul puts it this way:

for all have sinned and fall short of the glory of God.

Some people may believe they are morally good and that even though they aren't perfect, they certainly do not deserve hell. Yet when we compare our goodness with God's requirement for righteousness, we fall far short.

All of us have become like one who is unclean, and all our righteous acts are like filthy rags (Is. 64:6).

Regardless of how good you are, the Bible says your goodness is like dirty clothes. Sin has separated us from God.

Because the old sinful nature within us is against God. It never did obey God's laws and it never will (Rom. 8:7 TLB).

God is holy and requires righteousness of us

Only God is good and only He is perfect.

He [God] is the Rock, his works are perfect, and all his ways are just. A faithful God who does no wrong, upright and just is he (Deut 32:4 NIV).

Our sin has separated us from our perfect heavenly Father. We cannot meet God's righteous requirements.

But just as he who called you is holy, so be holy in all you do (1 Pet. 1:15).

Because He loves us, He made a provision for us.

The solution is Christ.

Jesus Christ made a way for us to be reconciled to God. Jesus was born of a virgin, so he was not corrupted by Adam's sin. Jesus is God because His Father is God.

For in Christ there is all of God in a human body (Col 2:9 TLB).

Jesus was born perfect and lived a perfect, sinless life so that He would be the perfect Sacrifice for our sin.

For God took the sinless Christ and poured into him our sins. Then, in exchange, he poured God's goodness into us! (2Cor 5:21 TLB).

Jesus took our sin upon Himself and was crucified so that we could be reunited with God. This demonstrates how much our Father God loves us!

For God so loved the world that he gave his one and only Son, that whoever believes in him shall not perish but have eternal life (John 3:16 NIV).

He rose from the dead on the third day to prove that He is God. No other religious leader has done this!

By being raised from the dead he was proved to be the mighty Son of God, with the holy nature of God himself (Rom. 1:4 TLB).

We must accept the salvation that Christ provides.

It isn't enough just to know that Jesus died for us. We must accept His sacrifice. We must acknowledge that we are sinners and that we need a Savior. We must ask Jesus to forgive us our sins, accept His sacrifice on the cross, and dedicate our life to Him.

You can do this now by praying this prayer from your heart. Keep in mind that it isn't the prayer that saves you—it is your heartfelt belief in the meaning of the prayer.

"Jesus, I am a sinner. Please forgive me of my sins.
I dedicate my life to you and I accept you as my
Savior and Lord. Amen."

Talk to God.

If you prayed this prayer and meant it, you are a Christian! You have been reunited with your loving heavenly Father. Why don't you take some time right now to talk with Him?

About the Author

For the past twenty years John Webster has ministered in churches, seminars and conferences in the United States and overseas. The core message of his ministry is teaching people how to hear God's voice.

John is founder/president of Transforming Life Ministry. He also served as the director of a Bible college and holds a bachelor's degree in theology and master's degree in biblical studies. John and his wife, Mary, live in Florida's panhandle area with their four children.

For more information, contact:
Transforming Life Ministry
P.O. Box 1360
Santa Rosa Beach, FL 323459
850-622-1780
life@transforminglife.org
www.transforminglife.org